MENTAL **MODELS**

How **understanding the mind** can transform the way you work and learn

JIM HEAL & REBEKAH BERLIN

Together we unlock every learner's unique potential

At Hachette Learning (formerly Hodder Education), there's one thing we're certain about. No two students learn the same way. That's why our approach to teaching begins by recognising the needs of individuals first.

Our mission is to allow every learner to fulfil their unique potential by empowering those who teach them. From our expert teaching and learning resources to our digital educational tools that make learning easier and more accessible for all, we provide solutions designed to maximise the impact of learning for every teacher, parent and student.

Aligned to our parent company, Hachette Livre, founded in 1826, we pride ourselves on being a learning solutions provider with a global footprint.

www.hachettelearning.com

To order, please visit www.HachetteLearning.com or contact Customer Service at education@hachette.co.uk / +44 (0)1235 827827.

ISBN: 978 1 3983 6968 9

First published in 2025 by
Hachette Learning,
An Hachette UK Company
Carmelite House
50 Victoria Embankment
London EC4Y 0DZ
www.HachetteLearning.com

The authorised representative in the EEA is Hachette Ireland, 8 Castlecourt Centre, Dublin 15, D15 XTP3, Ireland (email: info@hbgi.ie)

Impression 2
Year 2029 2028 2027 2026 2025

A catalogue record for this title is available from the British Library

Typeset in the UK
Printed in the UK

Jim

To my dad. Thank you for everything.

Rebekah

To Matt, who I even asked for feedback on this dedication.
You are an incredibly supportive partner.

Dr. Jim Heal is a leading advocate for bridging the worlds of research and practice through the applied science of learning. His work seeks to develop evidence-informed expertise in learning and leadership for schools, universities, and organizations around the world. He holds a Doctorate in Educational Leadership from Harvard University and is author of *How Teaching Happens* and *Instructional Illusions*.

Dr. Rebekah Berlin's research focuses on outcomes-oriented support for teachers and teacher-educators. Her work has included large-scale improvement efforts, change management, and the translation of research into practice. She currently works developing products to measure and improve the quality of interactions. Her Ph.D. is from University of Virginia.

REVIEWS

Understanding how the mind works transforms human performance, and *Mental Models* is the brilliant blueprint for that understanding. This book manages to take a complex, scientific understanding of the mind and plugs it into real-life examples that are at once practical, powerful, and essential to how we all learn. I don't know how else to say it: life-changing ideas are inside.

Holly Korbey, editor of The Bell Ringer, education journalist, and author of Building Better Citizens

What a book! In clear and non-jargon filled prose, Heal and Berlin open up the world of cognitive science. *Mental Models* makes cognitive science both accessible and actionable, offering a powerful framework for improving how we teach, lead, and learn. Essential for anyone looking to unlock the power of the mind in daily life.

Jal Mehta, Professor of Education at the Harvard Graduate School of Education and author of In Search of Deeper Learning

Mental Models brilliantly bridges the gap between research and real-world application, offering an accessible and actionable guide to how we think and learn. Heal and Berlin translate cognitive science into practical strategies that anyone—educators, leaders, and professionals can use to improve understanding, communication, and decision-making. A must-read for those looking to harness the power of the mind to drive meaningful impact.

Bridget Hamre, Cofounder and Chief Executive Officer at Teachstone and Associate Research Professor at the UVA School of Education and Human Development

The mental model is one of the most important concepts in teaching and learning. Experts understand ideas and make decisions quickly and effectively because they have a rich mental model—a blueprint in their mind of how a concept is supposed to look or work and why. But the critical question of how powerful mental models can be developed in learners is also poorly understood. This tremendously powerful book removes the mystery, providing practical steps educators can follow to understand mental models and help construct them optimally in the minds of learners. It is an exceptional contribution to the growing literature describing how cognitive science can and should inform learning.

Doug Lemov, author of Teach Like a Champion *and* Practice Perfect

Finally a book that clearly discusses mental models, what they are, and why they're important for teaching and learning. This book is a perfect combination of good science and what good science means for good learning. Heal and Berlin have an uncanny ability to make the most difficult concepts easy to understand. Their use of examples and analogies (two very powerful instructional techniques) serve as a 'hook' to capture your interest, as a 'facilitator' to make even the most difficult concepts easy to understand, and as an 'anchor' to help you to remember. A must for all teachers, educators, and trainers!

Paul A. Kirschner, Emeritus Professor of Educational Psychology, former President of the International Society for the Learning Sciences, and author of several books including How Learning Happens, How Teaching Happens, *and* Evidence Informed Learning Design

CONTENTS

INTRODUCTION

What makes some people succeed where others fail? Why do we experience success in some parts of our life but not others? Often, we attribute effectiveness to intangible qualities like "charisma" and "talent." We see great speakers and managers, and surmise that "they must have what it takes" without asking what "it" actually is. By the same token, whenever we strive to emulate others' successes and come up short, we're left thinking "it's just not for me." Such notions of ability and effectiveness stymie our growth and cause us to overlook factors that influence everyday human interactions, many of which are hiding in plain sight.

To consider what we mean, think of the last time you gave a presentation at work or tried teaching something to a child. What about the last time you led a team through a complex project or tried explaining a new idea to a friend? Now think of all the ways those situations may have gone awry: Countless hours preparing your presentation doesn't stop people asking about information you explicitly covered (were they even listening?); leading your team through a project goes from "finely oiled machine" to "herding cats" in what seems like no time at all; and attempting to explain something to your friend leaves you saying, "Actually, never mind. Don't worry about it."

Thankfully, we know that the likelihood of success in these, and a host of everyday interactions, can be improved by applying an understanding of our minds at work – otherwise known as *cognitive science*.

Cognitive science deals with how we make sense of the world, including how we attend to, process, and remember the information that makes up our lives. It can explain why people struggle to stay focused in presentations, why teams lose sight of an objective, and why it's notoriously difficult to explain an idea to someone when you know the concept all too well and they don't know where to start.

More importantly, cognitive science provides us with a roadmap that can help us be more effective more of the time, and that's what this book is all about.

Mental Models

So, what about the name of this book? Whether we're making a ham sandwich or playing a Beethoven sonata on the piano, most of us hold what cognitive scientists call "mental models" for how we go about doing a specific task. These mental representations allow us to see the whole, zoom in on individual parts, and consider the relationship between the two.

A mental model serves as a cognitive blueprint that guides our actions. When you floss your teeth, you might have a mental model that includes steps like: 1) wrapping each end of the floss around a finger; 2) starting in the bottom left quadrant and moving toward the bottom right; and 3) repeating with your top teeth. You can also probably play a movie of yourself going through these motions in your mind, with the ability to pause or zoom at any moment.

Mental models also serve as a reference point for our performance. Imagine you are cooking dinner, tasting along the way, and you realize it's under-salted. It's your mental model that is guiding you. It tells you what you *want* your dish to taste like, so you can keep adjusting the seasoning until you hit that bar.

We also refine our mental models over time. Your mental model of an effective pedal stroke is going to change if you are a toddler on a tricycle versus a pro cyclist in the Tour de France. With increasing expertise, our mental models become more accurate and often more complex.

While your mental model for how you floss your teeth or ride a bike may need no adjustment, most of our mental models need work. This is because much of what we do in the day-to-day involves complicated cognitive processes. And when we interact with others, we also have to contend with *their* cognitive processes, which only adds to the mess. To do this successfully, we need mental models informed by how the mind actually works, but there's a problem. Most of us operate with mental models that are informed not by research, but simply by what we've heard or seen others do.

As our examples suggest, two things can be said of cognitive science and its role in determining our daily successes or failures:

1. Our lives are full of opportunities to teach, learn, and grow with those around us.
2. Most of us don't recognize these opportunities as such. Even when we do, we're ill-prepared to apply an understanding of how the mind actually works to those moments.

In other words, we often enter into these situations with a particular mental model of success that is inadequate for the job at hand. We say to ourselves: This is what it takes to hold people's attention; this is what it looks like to set tangible objectives for a group; or this is what it takes to break down a concept for someone new to the idea. Our mental model for each of these acts (and countless more) could be enhanced by an understanding of how the mind works. However, despite massive strides in cognitive science over the last 50 or so years, most of us still go about our business unaware of its application to daily life.

The result of all these missed opportunities is clear: Nothing is taken away from the presentation; the team's work doesn't meet your standards; and the friend or family member walks away confused.

Refining Our Mental Models for Greater Effectiveness

If fostering growth in ourselves or supporting it in others were an intuitive act like learning to speak, this book wouldn't need to exist. In reality, refining one's mental models to align with principles of cognitive science is something closer to learning to read or write in that it demands a more intentional and systematic approach. Over the course of this book, we'll do just that by breaking down the cognitive processes that inform our daily activities.

- We'll start with **The Learning Mind** and introduce to you a model of cognition for everyday application. Here, we'll explore what happens in our minds when we encounter a new idea, process it, and (hopefully) remember it for future use.
- Then we'll encounter **The Ordered Mind** and see how experts' minds differ from those of novices, particularly in relation to the structure of long-term memory. We'll learn the role this plays in acquiring knowledge and how we make sense of the world around us, all with a focus on how to build understanding effectively.
- From there, we'll move on to **The Wheels of Cognition** to discover what has to happen if we want information to actually make it from our working memory into our long-term memory, why it often doesn't make it back out again, and what to do about it.
- We'll stop in on **The Weight of Thought** to understand cognitive load theory and learn how to "game" the learning process by managing the mental load we bear when we think.

- Finally, we'll explore **Journeys of the Mind** and put all the pieces of the learning process together. You'll leave with a coherent approach that can inform any situation where learning is the aim.

In all parts of our lives, we possess mental models for what we ought to do (or not) if we are to be effective and impactful. This book will guide you as you hone your mental models, preparing you to be more effective as you engage with the people and ideas that make up your life.

PART 1
THE LEARNING MIND: A MODEL OF COGNITION

This section sets the scene for what we mean when we talk about the mind, how it operates, and why that matters.

1. THE LEARNING MIND

Before we dive into different strategies you can use to harness cognitive processes to increase effectiveness, it's important to possess a mental model of how the mind actually works. We'll use this to ground the concepts to come.

Decades of research in cognitive science have coalesced into an understanding of how we think and learn. Daniel Willingham, a cognitive scientist at the University of Virginia, offered this simple version, which we'll reference throughout this book.

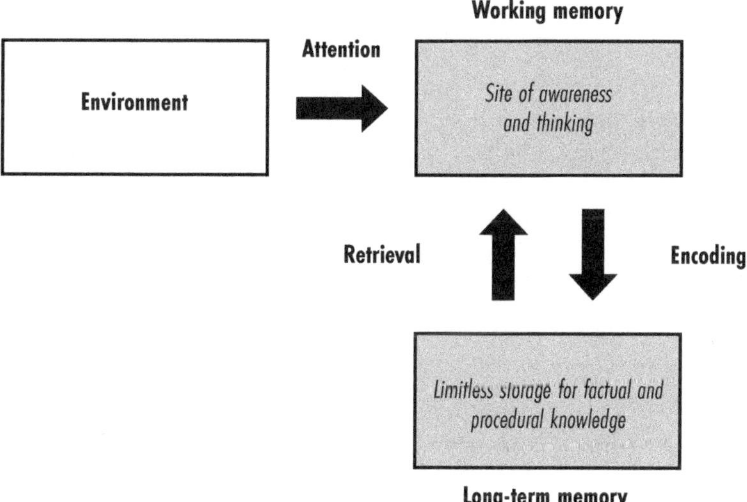

Here's the technical version. Information that we attend to is processed in working memory. From there we (hopefully) encode it into long-term memory where it can be stored indefinitely. When we need to access this information, we retrieve it back into working memory, the site of awareness and thinking. But what does this actually mean, and how might it play out in our daily lives?

Imagine it's your first week at a new job. As you exit the bathroom, you notice your manager in the hallway. Eager to make a good impression, you fall into step with her, and she tells you that a meeting has just been added to your calendar. It starts in 10 minutes. The meeting will be the two of you and some representatives from another organization that she wants to partner with. Just then, you feel your phone start to vibrate in your pocket. You quickly silence it, but after a few moments it starts vibrating again.

"Two calls back to back," you think. "Is there some kind of emergency? But what if I interrupt her to check and it's just a sales call?"

What's happening in this example? The moment the vibrations caught your attention, your working memory began to fill with thoughts ranging from "Why two calls? Is everyone okay?" to "How likely is it that it's my sister just calling to have something to do while she's driving to the grocery store?"

Here's the bad news. Attention and working memory are limited resources. The more you pay attention to one thing, the less you pay attention to something else.

So as your mind begins to fill with thoughts like "That better not be my sister, I asked her not to call me just to chat during the workday," your mind cannot also process the details your manager is sharing about the upcoming meeting. You might register that she's still talking and catch the occasional word, but your working memory is filled with strategizing a subtle way to slip your phone from your pocket to check who's calling.

Here's the other piece of bad news. The types of questions you are asking yourself, the type that cause you to a) elaborate on what could be prompting multiple calls and b) analyze the pros and cons of interrupting your boss to check your phone, those are the *exact* types of deep processing questions that prompt what cognitive scientists call "encoding."

Encoding is the process of moving information from working memory to long-term memory. Our working memory can only hold information for a few seconds, whereas our long-term memory can store it indefinitely. Information stays in long-term memory until we retrieve it for future use (remembering). Unless, of course, we forget. The experience of forgetting occurs when we don't have the right cues to recall the information. It also occurs when we don't use these cues and the memory traces – or paths by which we access the information – decay.

So, encoding is critical to being able to remember and use information. However, we can only encode what we first process in working memory. So if you want to remember your manager's reasons for why she's so invested in this potential partnership, your best bet is to deeply process the information. And if you spend that time, say, deeply processing the question "Are they calling because my house burned down? I turned the stove off, right?" then unfortunately, that's the only thing that's going to be available to you to pull from long-term memory later on.

Why does that matter? Well, imagine that after you'd determined it was two unfortunately timed sales calls, you walk into the meeting with your manager. Ten minutes in she gestures to you and says, "My new colleague is going to share a few of the reasons we find this potential partnership so exciting." Cast about as you may, the only thing you'll have available to pull from long-term memory related to your hallway exchange is the memory of nodding and saying "uh huh" at what you hoped were opportune moments in an attempt to distract from the fact that you were trying to shimmy your phone out of your pocket. Technically you "heard" what your manager was saying. You were present as your manager shared her thoughts in the hallway, and the sound waves reached your ear. However, because you didn't process what she was saying, it never made it into long-term memory. You can't remember why she's excited about the partnership, because you never attended to it in the first place.

Another way of thinking about this is to say the outcome of thinking is far from guaranteed. Our minds are constantly engaged in the process of attending to things in our environment, pulling information from long-term memory to make sense of them and processing all this in working memory. This process can go careening off the rails at every point: Working memory, encoding, long-term memory, and retrieval. And this has consequences. What and how we process has cascading effects on how we engage with others and our work.

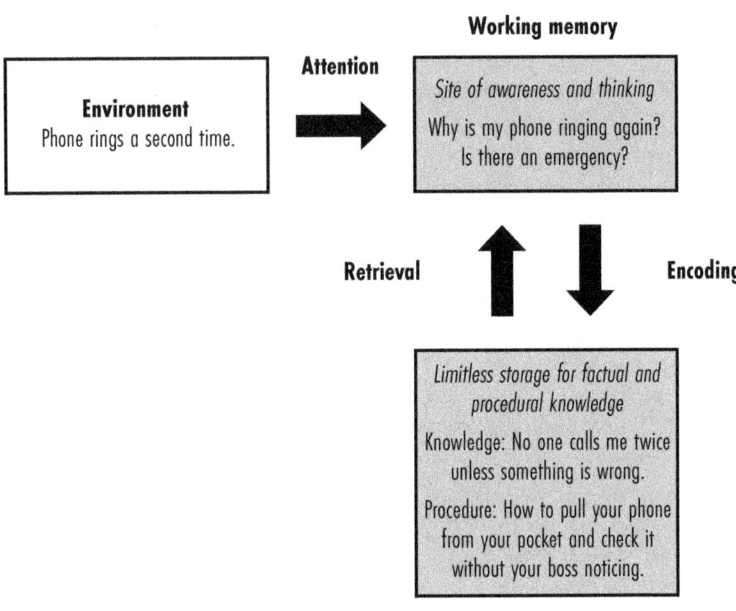

How does having a mental model of the mind help? When we understand how the mind works, we can shape and nudge mental processes for ourselves and others in ways that make it more likely we all achieve the outcomes we are looking for.

Let's run this same example back, this time showing how an understanding of the mind might impact the outcome. Imagine it's your first week at a new job. As you exit the bathroom, you notice your manager in the hallway. Eager to make a good impression, you fall into step with her, and she tells you that a meeting has just been added to your calendar that starts in 10 minutes. It will be the two of you and some representatives from another organization that she is keen to partner with. Just then, you feel your phone start to vibrate in your pocket. You quickly silence it, but after a few moments it starts vibrating again.

Noticing you seem momentarily distracted, your manager pauses until you look back at her. Then she says, "My question for you is, how do we help them see their goals align with ours?"

Responding to this question immediately kicks off the type of deep processing that makes it likely you'll be able to remember information later. Knowing that your working memory is limited, you understand you can't simultaneously grapple with prepping for an impromptu, important meeting and questions about the implications of your phone continuing to vibrate. You tell yourself, "I'll check as soon as I'm at my desk," and allow the thoughts of your phone to pass out of working memory. This opens space in working memory to focus on your manager's question.

After responding, you listen to her list the reasons she is eager for the two organizations to partner. You agree, but silently ask yourself another deep processing question: "I get why this would be good for our organization, but why would they want to partner with us?" Back at your desk, you glance at your phone, confirm it is back-to-back sales calls and refocus. You jot down a response that incorporates your manager's rationale as well as information you gathered about both organizations during your job search that you pull from long-term memory.

That jogs a memory of a partnership meeting at your previous organization. While that organization had a different focus than your current one, you consider which parts of the process you used to support partnerships there might be useful in this context. You add a few examples of projects the two organizations could partner onto your notes and walk into the meeting ready for anything your manager throws your way.

What made these hallway interactions and their outcomes so different? Obviously, there was a bit more emotional regulation in the second version. But the primary difference is how different the thinking process was at every step of the way.

Working memory

Environment
Phone rings a second time.

Attention

Site of awareness and thinking

Why is my phone ringing again?
Is there an emergency?

Retrieval

Encoding

Limitless storage for factual and procedural knowledge

Knowledge: No one calls me twice unless something is wrong.

Procedure: How to pull your phone from your pocket and check it without your boss noticing.

Long-term memory

Working memory

Environment
Phone rings a second time.
Boss says, "My question for you is, how do we help them see their goals align with ours?"

Attention

Site of awareness and thinking

How do we help them see their goals align with ours?

Why would they want to partner with us?

Retrieval

Encoding

Limitless storage for factual and procedural knowledge

Knowledge:
- Information about each organization.
- Similarities between this partnership and partnership at previous workplace.
- Partnership strategies.

Long-term memory

In the first version, working memory and later long-term memory were filled with thoughts like "To check or not to check the phone?" In the second, the entire process was focused on processing information that could prove critical to the success of a high-stakes meeting.

Like bumpers in a bowling alley, when we possess a mental model of how the mind works, we can provide deliberate nudges that keep the process headed in the direction we want it to go. When your manager paused when you seemed distracted, she wasn't just being polite. She was giving you a chance to refocus your attention on what turned out to be the most important information at hand. When she asked you to respond to the question "How do we help them see their goals align with ours?" she prompted the exact type of thinking that makes it most likely you'll remember the answer later (just as you did when you later asked yourself, "Why would they want to partner with us?").

Obviously, most of us don't spend our time at work refining our ability to check our phones during a conversation without others noticing (well, maybe a little). But chances are you do find yourself in meetings, giving presentations, training someone new, managing projects, leading teams, or in a variety of situations where people are thinking and growing together. All of these are thinking and learning processes.

Rather than leave these to chance, we can use the principles of cognitive science to make them more effective. We'll begin diving into these principles in the next chapter.

Takeaways

- Working memory is a limited resource. The more we attend to and process one thing, the less we can attend to and process something else.
- Encoding (information moving from working to long-term memory) is not a given. Without it, there's no remembering, so fix the odds in your favor. Deep processing (analyzing, elaborating, justifying) makes remembering more likely.
- Working memory is limited. Long-term memory is limitless.
- Remembering is nothing more than retrieving information from long-term memory to working memory.

References and further reading

Altmann, E. M., & Gray, W. D. (2002). Forgetting to remember: The functional relationship of decay and interference. *Psychological Science, 13*(1), 27–33.

Atkinson, R. C., & Shiffrin, R. M. (1968). Human memory: A proposed system and its control processes. In *Psychology of Learning and Motivation* (Vol. 2). New York: Academic Press, pp. 89–195.

Bransford, J. D., Brown, A. L., & Cocking, R. R. (2000). *How People Learn* (Vol. 11). Washington, DC: National Academy Press.

Chandler, P., & Sweller, J. (1991). Cognitive load theory and the format of instruction. *Cognition and Instruction, 8*(4), 293–332.

Chincotta, D., Underwood, G., Ghani, K. A., Papadopoulou, E., & Wresinski, M. (1999). Memory span for arabic numerals and digit words: Evidence for a limited-capacity, visuospatial storage system. *Quarterly Journal of Experimental Psychology Section A, 52*(2), 325–351.

Ericsson, K. A., & Kintsch, W. (1995). Long-term working memory. *Psychological Review, 102*(2), 211–245.

Willingham, D. T. (2017). A mental model of the learner: Teaching the basic science of educational psychology to future teachers. *Mind, Brain, and Education, 11*(4), 166–175.

Willingham, D. T., & Riener, C. (2019). *Cognition: The Thinking Animal.* Cambridge: Cambridge University Press.

PART 2

THE ORDERED MIND: THE STRUCTURE OF LONG-TERM MEMORY

This section offers an introduction to long-term memory, its role, and its structure. We will focus on three ways you can ensure people have the information they need in long-term memory and can flexibly apply it.

2. SHOW AND TELL: PAIR THE ABSTRACT WITH THE CONCRETE

Wild though this might be to consider, imagine for a moment that a pandemic is sweeping the globe. As both scientists and the public attempt to internalize what is happening, the challenge of how to communicate the terms of something that none of us has experienced before becomes ever more real.

Now imagine a disconnect between the scientists and the wider population, not in terms of credibility (though this would likely be a significant factor) but instead of basic understanding. Granted, the public has a commonsense appreciation of illnesses and how they spread, and the scientists have expertise in communicable disease and a growing appreciation of this particular virus – but this doesn't immunize either group from misunderstanding each other. Indeed, just because the public *think* they understand how diseases spread in general doesn't mean they will fully comprehend the rate at which this virus will propagate. Similarly, just because the scientists are experts in their own domain doesn't mean they are capable of explaining what's happening in ways that everyday people will understand.

Consider for instance what it would mean for the public at large to understand a statement like "This virus is growing *exponentially*." When attempting to explain the concept, scientists might rely on euphemisms like "It's spreading like wildfire" but that clearly doesn't capture the full story. Incidentally, exponential growth bias is a real phenomenon. Researchers have found it's the reason we're more likely to apply for that new credit card, because we intuitively underestimate the impact of compound interest on savings and loans. It's also the reason we might underestimate a virus' potential to become widespread *very* quickly.

What explains the disconnect in cases such as these? The problem lies in the fact that terms like "exponential" are abstract concepts, especially when background knowledge is limited. Abstract concepts are too easy to generalize and are therefore more liable to remain vague or underdeveloped in our minds. For instance, even if an average person understands that "exponential" relates to rapid growth, that doesn't mean they have a grasp of exactly what the rate of growth of a communicable disease looks like in real terms – that is *unless* we anchor the concept in a reality people can access and understand.

So, what to do about this disconnect? How do we communicate concepts in ways that reveal their fullness and avoid misunderstanding-by-abstraction? We do so by pairing such abstract concepts (new terms, metaphors, big ideas) with concrete examples that ground the idea and lend it substance. How to do that well will be the stuff of this chapter.

When Experts and Novices Collide

To understand the importance of pairing abstract concepts with concrete examples, we must first understand the difference between experts and novices. One common misconception about novices is that they approach problems or encounter information in much the same way as experts. It turns out that the reality is quite different, and thanks to cognitive science, we are able to demonstrate how.

We have come to understand that experts not only have more knowledge at their disposal than novices, but the manner in which they organize what they know is more sophisticated. This is because an expert doesn't see information as a series of isolated facts but rather as a network of interrelated concepts, which cognitive scientists refer to as a schema.

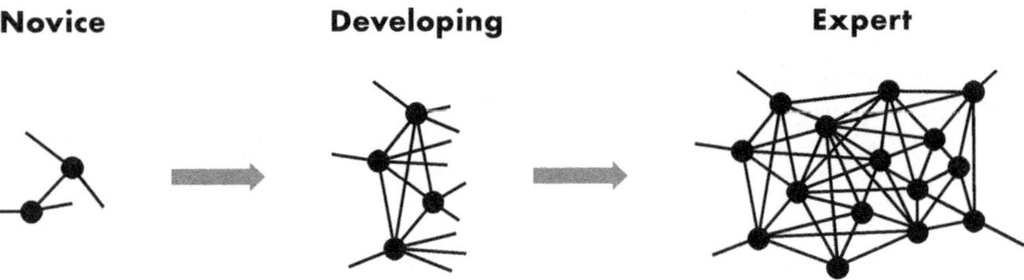

We all develop schemas in one way or another over time. A schema at its most fundamental is the reason even a child is able to name categorical similarities and differences between a cat and a dog. Jim's 4-year-old can see how cats and dogs both have four legs and fur, but that there are other things that draw them apart (e.g. one meows while the other woofs).

Now, imagine what it would look like if Nora went on in adulthood to achieve a degree in zoology with a concentration in the comparative biologies of feline and canine species. Her ability to see the fine-grained differences between what makes a cat a cat and a dog a dog would be unrecognizably advanced by comparison. Her schemas in relation to these concepts would be richer, more rounded, more connected. For instance, Nora might go on to learn that cats cannot produce certain essential amino acids, so they must eat meat or fish in order to stay healthy, and since dogs don't have that deficiency, they can technically live without meat or fish. Therefore, dogs can be vegetarians but cats cannot. Notice the difference here is not simply "more facts" but rather a more sophisticated appreciation of the relationship between parts of knowledge and how they fit together.

This question of what stands experts' schemas apart from those of novices has been explored by cognitive scientists in experimental conditions for decades. In one study conducted in 1973 by Chase and Simon, three groups (novice chess players, class A players, and chess grandmasters) were shown a snapshot of a chess game and given five seconds to memorize the positions of the pieces. After five seconds the board was once again covered and participants had to recall the configuration as precisely as possible. This process was repeated until each participant achieved perfect recall of all the pieces on the board.

As you might expect, the novice chess players required more attempts to memorize the positions of the pieces than their class A player counterparts, and the class A players needed more attempts to memorize the board than the grandmasters. At this point, the researchers made an ingenious shift to the terms of the experiment. They placed the chess pieces in an entirely random configuration so that the positions did not resemble an actual game of chess. In this new configuration the grandmasters did no better than the class A players, or even the novices for that matter, when it came to remembering where the pieces were placed.

Through this work, researchers were able to show that the grandmasters didn't possess a better memory than the other participants who were mere mortals in chess terms. Instead, the grandmasters were able to draw on the vast repertoire of chess piece configurations they had encountered over years of practice and game play: A repertoire that was organized into a contextually specific understanding of the typical patterns one might find within a game. This is why they remembered real chess piece positions so well but could not repeat that feat when unconventional chess scenarios were on display.

So, as you can see, experts don't just know more than novices. They observe and organize information differently.

Experts "Cut to the Chase" More Quickly than Novices

Developing a more sophisticated schema and seeing knowledge as a pattern of ideas is advantageous because it enables experts to cue in to the right aspects of a concept and determine what's most worthy of attention. This comes in handy when solving problems, as shown in this example from a 1993 essay by Katherine K. Merseth:

> There are 125 sheep and five dogs in a flock. How old is the shepherd?

Like most adults reading this book, you were likely able to realize at first glance that this question relies on a nonsensical premise and is impossible to answer. You might therefore be surprised to learn that three out of four school-age children who were asked this question attempted to solve it, with many even providing a numerical response and accompanying rationale. Here, a transcript from the study reveals the thought process one student used to arrive at their answer:

> 125 + 5 = 130 is too big, and 125 - 5 = 120 is still too big, while 125 ÷ 5 = 25. That works! I think the shepherd is 25 years old.

As you can see, the novice is unable to cue in to the most pertinent information on display (this is an unsolvable question) and therefore expends unnecessary cognitive energy (plugging in numbers until they arrive at a "plausible" answer) in an attempt to solve the unsolvable. This is a cognitively costly act – especially when you consider the finite nature of working memory and how easy it is to slip into cognitive overload – and sadly it's a cognitive flaw we pay the price of *all the time* in our everyday lives. Indeed, there's a reason why we talk about "paying" attention to something, because all attention comes at a cost. As such, knowing what's most worthy of attention is a key indicator of expertise, and it turns out expertise is a great way of cutting cognitive costs.

So, how do we help novices to lower the cognitive price they must pay in understanding something new? That's where concrete examples come into play.

Experts, Novices, and the Power of Concrete Examples

Despite all their obvious strengths, being an expert does not guarantee that you'll be effective at explaining what you know to non-experts. As you might already be intuiting, this is because experts have arrived at a level of sophistication that makes it hard for them to remember the challenges that same topic might present to a novice. Or to put it another way, experts tend to forget what non-expertise feels like.

Thankfully, there is hope for experts, or anyone hoping to convey an idea to the uninitiated, and it's got something to do with how we exemplify our thinking. We know from research into cognitive science that humans are predisposed to understand concrete expressions of concepts more than abstract representations, and it turns out that combining the two has powerful properties for understanding and durable learning.

In a 1994 study, a team of researchers led by Allan Paivio presented participants with factual paragraphs about historical figures. Each paragraph was scored by participants in relation to familiarity (I have seen some version of this information before) and concreteness (this information is presented with concrete examples rather than abstract ideas alone).

Specifically, the study acknowledged the differing conditions of the paragraph sets as follows:

- **Set 1:** Two paragraphs rated **equal in familiarity** but **one paragraph rated as more concrete than the other**.
- **Set 2:** Two paragraphs **differing in both familiarity and concreteness**, with the **less concrete paragraph rated as the more familiar of the two**.

In the case where the concrete and abstract paragraphs were equally familiar, participants recalled the concrete paragraph nearly twice as well. In the case where the abstract paragraph was more familiar, participants recalled the paragraphs equally well. In other words, the concreteness of the content supercharged their ability to learn the information on display and was still effective, even when that information was less familiar to them.

So, whenever an expert starts to fall into the trap of assuming a novice holds the same sophisticated schemas as they do, concrete examples can help illustrate the concept at work. We know this to be valuable because concepts presented in concrete terms are easier for us to access, understand, and remember.

A simple example of this can be found by returning to a question we invoked at the very beginning of this chapter: "How might an expert demonstrate to a novice the idea that viruses spread at exponential rates?"

A straightforward dictionary definition of the word "exponential" would read as something like "(of an increase) becoming more and more rapid," while a mathematical definition might be "involving a variable in an exponent." However, by now we know that is too abstract.

So, let's try this instead. Imagine an expert presenting what they mean by "a virus that spreads exponentially" as follows:

Exponential is a term used to describe the growth of something that is proportional to its current size. This is different to linear growth, which simply involves adding the same amount each time (e.g. 2, 4, 6, 8, 10, etc.), exponential growth increases the amount of change each time. To understand how exponential growth can be shocking in cases like the spread of a virus, consider the following example:

Picture a large pond that is empty except for one lily pad. Now picture that lily pad doubling in number every day for 48 days until the pond is completely covered. As surprising as this might seem, the pond will only be ***half covered*** *on the 47th day. It would only take the final day of growth for the pond to go from half covered to entirely overrun with lily pads.*

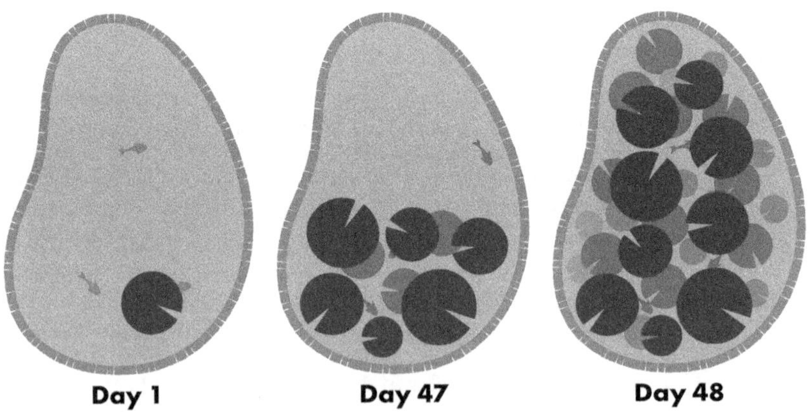

This is what makes exponential growth in the case of a virus so surprising. The rate it spreads is gradual at first but accelerates explosively. You can go from half the population infected to the entire population in a single day.

Approaches like this work because they invite the learner to tighten the bond between the concept and what it actually means. Coming to understand an idea requires a learner to understand what it looks and sounds like in real life and establish meaningful connections between these examples and the more general concept. All of which brings us to the first of our mental models.

Concrete Examples in Practice

Big Idea: Ideas expressed abstractly can be difficult for novice learners to understand, so we should pair generalities with concrete examples.

Mental Model: Show and Tell.

We all remember "show and tell" day at school. The idea was simple: You were tasked with bringing an object to show your classmates and explain what it represented. At its heart, the pairing of abstract concepts with concrete examples is no different, and here's how you can do it for yourself.

Step 1: What's the Thing You Want to "Tell"?

This might appear simple at first, but we often don't realize which topics are more accessible versus which are more abstract. We therefore need to define our content clearly so we can complement them with clarifying, memorable examples.

Let's say for example that you're delivering a session to your work colleagues on how change happens in organizations. Specifically, your plan is to introduce them to a model for change that you think will be helpful: Adaptive versus technical challenges. You happen to know that your colleagues have not encountered the idea before, and since you know the concept is a tricky one, you want to make absolutely certain that they can internalize it before applying it to their own work. Here is a dictionary-style definition of the concepts you're hoping to convey:

- **Technical challenges** are those aspects of an individual or organization that are ready for change. For a technical challenge, it's likely that you and/or your team already know what they need to know and have the required resources, and all that needs to happen is for everyone to execute the plan.
- **Adaptive challenges** are those aspects of an individual or organization that are resistant to change. For an adaptive challenge, it's likely that you and/or your team don't know what you need to know and don't have the required resources, and therefore if something about the situation is going to change then something about you and your team is going to have to change.

Now that you have established the core of the idea you want to convey, and the parts that newcomers might need support in understanding, it's time to move to the next step.

Step 2: How Will You "Show" What You Mean?

As with any good show and tell, the trick to this step lies in selecting the right example. You need one that makes the core content more accessible and memorable.

In this case, a concrete example that maps onto the most important features of adaptive versus technical challenges would look something like this:

Feature of the Core Idea	Concrete Example Representing the Idea
Technical challenges assume that the solution to the problem already exists and that all you need to do is execute your plan.	Imagine you visit your doctor for a routine check-up, and they tell you for the first time that your blood pressure is high for your age. Knowing that this can be an early warning sign for heart disease and other ailments later in life, you decide to do something about it. • A technical articulation of the challenge would be: "I have high blood pressure." • A technical solution to this challenge would therefore simply say: "I'm going to visit my doctor and have them prescribe me a drug to help me lower my blood pressure." In this technical conception of the problem, you see your blood pressure as a straightforward problem with a straightforward solution, when in reality it's more complex. If taking the pill was **all** you did to address the problem, without considering how else you might need to change, then your chances of lowering your blood pressure and keeping it that way would suffer.
Adaptive challenges assume that the solution to the problem does not yet exist, which therefore requires you to do things differently than before.	Let's still imagine you wish to lower your blood pressure but instead take the adaptive approach. • An adaptive articulation of the challenge would be: "I am making life choices that are leading to high blood pressure." • An adaptive solution to this challenge would therefore say: "I'm going to change my lifestyle and monitor what works. I will do this until I figure out the right combination of exercise, medication, and stress management to lower my blood pressure."

Step 3: How Will You Engage Your Listeners in the "Show and Tell"?

This is where you bring it all together. Rather than seeing the concept and its concrete examples as separate entities, you should now ask yourself: "How can I communicate the core concept via my well-selected examples?"

As we know from the previous chapter on the learning mind, we know that information that is not attended to and processed will not be successfully encoded into long-term memory. As such, you need to cue learners to the idea, to the example of it, and to the relationship between the two. In this case, that would look like: "How is each of these examples representative of adaptive versus technical approaches to change?"

Subsequent steps could then invite people to come up with their own examples before holding them up to the concept upon which the example is based (e.g. "Think of a time when we were able to be adaptive – what did that look like? Now think of a time when we were more technically minded – what did that look like? What conditions prompted us to adopt one approach over the other?")

Conclusion

To paraphrase Oliver Wendell Holmes, concrete examples provide "simplicity on the other side of complexity" in that they offer insights into the underlying architecture of ideas. By showing as well as telling, such examples provide us with a cognitive hook upon which to hang our hat; a representation to which we can return when the overall complexity of the idea might require regrounding. What's more, the pairing of concrete examples with generalized concepts strengthens the bond between big ideas and their lived reality, making them more concrete, accessible, and memorable.

Takeaways

- Experts and novices handle knowledge differently. While novices are more likely to see knowledge items in isolated units, experts increasingly see knowledge as part of an interconnected network of ideas known as a schema.
- Having more sophisticated schemas means experts can draw on a repertoire of representational examples to make sense of what they see, as well as being quicker to differentiate between more- and less-meaningful informational details.
- Being an expert does not guarantee that you'll be effective at explaining what you know to non-experts. Specific examples help. Research has shown that pairing abstract concepts with concrete examples makes that information more accessible and memorable, so use a "show and tell" approach to explain and exemplify ideas.

References and further reading

Chase, W. G., & Simon, H. A. (1973). Perception in chess. *Cognitive Psychology, 4*(1), 55–81.

Clark, J. M., & Paivio, A. (1991). Dual coding theory and education. *Educational Psychology Review, 3*, 149–210.

Lang, T., & Ramirez, R. (2020). *Tending the lily pond: Exponential growth and scenario planning*. Saïd Business School. Available at: www.sbs.ox.ac.uk/oxford-answers/tending-lily-pond-exponential-growth-and-scenario-planning (Accessed: November 25, 2024).

Merseth, K. K. (1993). How old is the shepherd? An essay about mathematics education. *Phi Delta Kappan, 74*(7), 548–554.

National Research Council. (2000). *How People Learn: Brain, Mind, Experience, and School: Expanded Edition*. Washington, DC: The National Academies Press.

Paivio, A., Walsh, M., & Bons, T. (1994). Concreteness effects on memory: When and why? *Journal of Experimental Psychology: Learning, Memory, and Cognition, 20*(5), 1196–1204.

Reusser, K. (1988). Problem solving beyond the logic of things: Contextual effects on understanding and solving word problems. *Instructional Science, 17*(4), 309–338.

Sabers, D. S., Cushing, K. S., & Berliner, D. C. (1991). Differences among teachers in a task characterized by simultaneity, multidimensionality, and immediacy. *American Educational Research Journal, 28*(1), 63–88.

Sadoski, M., Kealy, W. A., Goetz, E. T., & Paivio, A. (1997). Concreteness and imagery effects in the written composition of definitions. *Journal of Educational Psychology, 89*(3), 518–526.

Sadoski, M., & Paivio, A. (2004). A dual coding theoretical model of reading. In R. B. Ruddell & N. J. Unrau (eds.) *Theoretical Models and Processes of Reading* (5th ed.). Newark, DE: International Reading Association, pp. 1329–1362.

Weinstein, Y. (2019). *Learn to study using...concrete examples*. The Learning Scientists. Available at: https://www.learningscientists.org/blog/2016/8/25-1 (Accessed: November 25, 2024).

3. MORE IS MORE: BUILD RICH SCHEMAS VIA VARIED EXAMPLES

What is a fork? This ought to be a straightforward question but try asking Maria Argyropoulina, the people at her wedding, or Ariel in Disney's *The Little Mermaid*. You'd find three very different answers (respectively, a utensil, an instrument of the devil, and a comb). We'll explore why in this chapter on varied examples and their relationship to building schemas.

Humans have a long history of having limited ideas on what things mean and how things ought to be done. At her wedding in 1004, Maria Argyropoulina shocked guests when she opened a small case and pulled out a golden fork, which she used throughout her wedding feast. Maria, the niece of the Byzantine emperors Basil II and Constantine VIII, was marrying the son of the Doge of Venice and her Venetian guests were horrified. So horrified that when she died a few years later Saint Peter Damian proclaimed the fork was an instrument of the devil, saying that when Maria ate, "she would impale on a certain golden instrument with two prongs and thus carry to her mouth ... this woman's vanity was hateful to Almighty God; and so, unmistakably, did He take his revenge." The result? Forks weren't used in Europe for the next 400 years. In fact, it wasn't until 1633 that English nobility came around when Charles I proclaimed, "It is decent to use a fork."

While blackballing a utensil for half a century may sound extreme, research from cognitive scientists would suggest we shouldn't be surprised. Without exposure to different examples of what something is or can be used for, we're likely to have limited schemas that constrain us.

Using Multiple Examples to Identify the Deep Structure

As we discussed in chapter 2, our long-term memory is filled with knowledge and processes that are organized into schemas. A schema is often represented as concept nodes with connected features and examples.

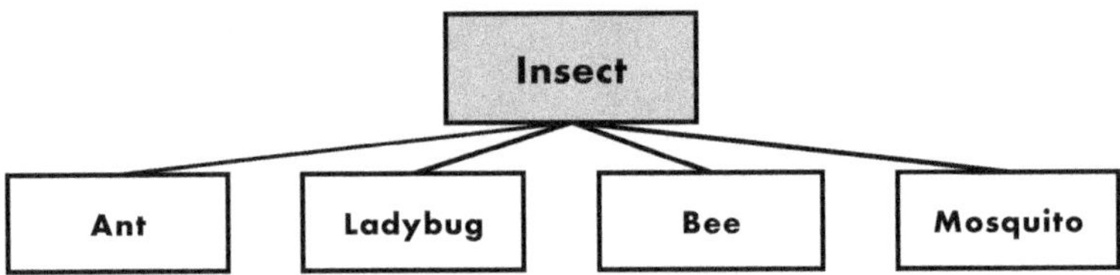

We also discussed how schemas of novices and experts differ in a few important ways. First, experts tend to have more robust schemas than novices – they have a lot more details about each concept stored in long-term memory. Second, experts can decipher which details related to a concept are most important to pay attention to. They can identify the deep structure. For example, if I ask, "What is Velcro?" an expert would describe the deep structure: Two strips – one with a series of loops, one with a series of hooks – that can stick together. A novice might describe surface features that are not core to the concept or not always true (e.g. often on kids' shoes, white).

Cognitive scientists have found that in order to learn something new, novices benefit from three things:

1. Exposure to multiple, varied examples
2. Support in understanding the relationship between the big idea and each example
3. Support in understanding the relationship between the examples themselves.

Here's what we mean by that (and why we mentioned Velcro earlier). In the 1940s, Swiss engineer George de Mestral went for a walk with his dog. Upon returning home he noticed his clothes were covered in burrs. Curious, he looked at the burrs under a microscope and noticed they were covered in a series of hooks that attached themselves to loops in the fabric of his clothing. He began experimenting with ways to create a hook and loop system, and Velcro was born.

If you showed someone who hadn't heard this story a burr and a strip of Velcro and gave them 30 seconds to share what, if anything, they have in common, you might hear: "Not much. One is found in nature and is brown. The other is manmade and often found on clothing. I guess they both sometimes stick to stuff you don't want them to?" This person would be tuning in to the surface features.

Now imagine asking a person who had a schema for the deep structure stored in long-term memory. Almost instantly they'd say, "A hook and loop system."

So how do we help someone deeply understand the deep structure of a concept? We provide them several, varied examples and then ask them questions to help them identify the deep structure. In the example above, if we are trying to help someone understand the concept of a hook and loop system, we'd first show them two examples: A burr and a piece of Velcro. Then we might say, "These two items appear different on the surface but they are actually very similar. You said they both sometimes stick to stuff you don't want them to. Why is that? What structural similarities do they share? They don't stick to everything. What do the things they stick to have in common?" The first two questions would help them note the hooks and the third question would help them note the loops, which together make up the deep structure.

So, describing the relationship between two examples can help people identify the deep structure of a concept, but is two examples enough? Why do we say we need multiple, varied examples?

Typicality Effects

Studies have repeatedly shown that the examples we associate most with a category are those with which we are most familiar. Imagine someone is talking about herbs and the one you've encountered most is parsley. Not only is it likely to come to mind, you'll also think it's the "truer" example of a culinary herb than ones you are less familiar with. That is, you'll think of parsley as more "herby" than watercress, even if you are told both are herbs. Researchers call this a "typicality effect." It's also why if you say "culinary herbs" and ask people to generate examples, the first thing that comes out of their mouth will likely be an example of herbs used in the food they grew up with or what they cook with now.

This is where varied examples come in. If instead of only occasionally seeing parsley, you grew up cooking with watercress, Thai basil, Italian basil, lemongrass, papalo, purslane, cilantro, oregano, thyme, rosemary, lavender, and different types of sage, you'll have a lot more examples to pull from in long-term memory and you'll be less likely to think one is a better example than another. Your schema is rich and nuanced.

There's a dark side to this phenomenon. People's schemas and the examples that they can call to mind easily are heavily influenced by what they encounter on a day-to-day basis. This is one of the ways that people develop biases and buy into stereotypes. For example, if children never see examples of Black women running organizations, and instead only see examples of White men in executive roles, they may incorrectly assume that White men are the only people who can run a company – that being a White man is somehow part of the deep structure of being an executive.

Advertisers know this well. To reduce the chance you'll think there's only one "type" of person that can use their product, they'll invest heavily in ad campaigns that show lots of different users (older, younger, different racial identities, different family statuses, different gender identities, etc.). Follow their lead. If we want to build robust, accurate schemas and to counter the tendency to generalize what we see most often into the "best" examples of something, we need to repeatedly expose ourselves (and others) to varied examples. This limits the chance we get an overly limited idea of what something is.

Functional Fixedness

Cognitive scientists have also discovered a phenomenon called "functional fixedness." This is our unfortunate tendency to think inflexibly; most of the time, we only think of uses for an object that we've encountered before. For example, if you are trying to pound a nail into a wall, the only object you'll think to use is a hammer when actually the back of a wrench could probably do the job in a pinch.

Let's return to our opening question, "What is a fork?" Functional fixedness (or lack thereof) is what makes Ariel in Disney's *The Little Mermaid* such an anomaly. Unburdened by fixed ideas of what a fork is or what it can be used for, she uses it as a comb. If we want people to think as flexibly as Ariel, we need to ensure they have enough varied examples in their schemas that they won't get stuck with limited ideas of how things ought to be done. Providing people with varied examples ensures they are working from accurate information and are set up to be independent, creative problem solvers. All of which brings us to our next mental model.

More is More in Practice

Big Idea: Use varied examples to develop rich, nuanced schemas and avoid overgeneralizing.

Mental Model: Build a Three-Legged Stool.

Here's one way you can actually put what researchers have learned about the power of multiple, varied examples into practice.

Imagine you are building a three-legged stool with someone anytime you are introducing something new.

Build the Seat: Introduce the General Concept

Firmly situate yourself in the seat of the idea. Say you want to give feedback to someone who reports to you. Start by introducing the general idea: You want them to show more initiative.

Build the Legs: Prop Up Your Idea By Providing at Least Three Examples

Prioritize examples that are most important for them in the near-term. Remember typicality effects – if they encounter it often (e.g. hearing from you), they'll likely think of it easily. Prioritize examples that will combat biases.

After you say you want them to show more initiative, prop up your statement by providing at least three examples of what you hope that will look like: Creating agendas for upcoming meetings; following up on action items without prompting; and generating suggestions for how to make existing processes more efficient.

Build to Last: Ask Questions That Strengthen the Connection

Ensure the new information sticks by creating a strong connection between examples and the broader takeaway. The sentence stem "Why is ___ also an example of this?" can help people articulate the deep structure. There's no need to stop at three examples. Strengthen their understanding (and check they are taking away what you want them to) by asking them to generate additional examples.

In this example, you might ask them to generate a couple of other examples of ways they could show initiative in their role. You could also provide an example they might not have thought of and help them connect it back to the concept of taking initiative. For example, you might ask, "How could asking for feedback be a great additional example of showing initiative?"

Why This Helps

Compare that to a manager who gives feedback by saying, "I'd like you to show more initiative," and stops there. This is too abstract to be useful. Without examples, everything is open to interpretation. For example, the person who reports to you might hear that and think, "Ah, they want me to talk more," when actually you want them to proactively come to you when they have questions.

It also won't work to just give one example. If you only say, "I'd like you to show more initiative, like creating agendas," they may create an agenda and think, "Agenda made. I've mastered taking initiative." With this overly limited conception of what "taking initiative" means, that may be the only change in their behavior. If instead you provide additional examples, you set them up to see the deep structure and think, "Oh, this isn't just about meetings..." You're tuning them in to the multiple uses of the fork.

Conclusion

People tend to anchor on what they've seen, and not in a good way. If we want them to develop nuanced schemas that allow for flexible problem solving, we have to give them varied examples.

Takeaways

- We tend to think in limited ways. Most of the time, we only generate uses for an object that we've encountered before. The examples we associate most with a category and those we think of as "best" tend to be those with which we are most familiar.
- Use varied examples to counter bias and nip stereotyping in the bud. Help people build nuanced schemas by making sure at least one example you share is something they are unlikely to generate on their own.
- Expand schemas by having people generate their own examples of a new idea. Just make sure they can explain *why* they are accurate examples of a particular concept or process. A great sentence stem is "Why is ___ a good example of that?"

References and further reading

Atkinson, R. K., Derry, S. J., Renkl, A., & Wortham, D. (2000). Learning from examples: Instructional principles from the worked examples research. *Review of Educational Research, 70*(2), 181–214.

Azzarito, A. (2020). *'A tool of the devil': The dark history of the humble fork.* Fast Company. Available at: www.fastcompany.com/90481445/a-tool-of-the-devil-the-dark-history-of-the-humble-fork (Accessed: November 26, 2024).

Azzarito, A. (2020). *Ten surprising facts about everyday household objects.* Smithsonian Magazine. Available at: www.smithsonianmag.com/innovation/ten-surprising-facts-about-everyday-household-objects-180974566/ (Accessed: November 26, 2024).

Hilbert, T. S., Schworm, S. I. L. K. E., & Renkl, A. (2004). Learning from worked-out examples: The transition from instructional explanations to self-explanation prompts. *Instructional Design for Effective and Enjoyable Computer-Supported Learning*, 184–192.

Proffitt, J. B., Coley, J. D., & Medin, D. L. (2000). Expertise and category-based induction. *Journal of Experimental Psychology: Learning, Memory, and Cognition, 26*(4), 811–828.

Quilici, J. L., & Mayer, R. E. (1996). Role of examples in how students learn to categorize statistics word problems. *Journal of Educational Psychology, 88*(1), 144–161.

Rosch, E. H. (1975). Cognitive representations of semantic categories. *Journal of Experimental Psychology: General, 104*(3), 192–233.

Salvi, C., Bricolo, E., Franconeri, S. L., Kounios, J., & Beeman, M. (2015). Sudden insight is associated with shutting out visual inputs. *Psychonomic Bulletin & Review, 22*, 1814–1819.

Smithsonian Institute. (2014). *George de Mestral: Velcro® inventor.* Available at: https://invention.si.edu/george-de-mestral-velcro-inventor (Accessed: November 26, 2024).

Willingham, D. T., & Riener, C. (2019). *Cognition: The Thinking Animal.* Cambridge: Cambridge University Press.

4. HERE'S WHAT I DON'T MEAN: USING NON-EXAMPLES

When Rebekah was in her early teens, her dad told her it was time for her to start mowing the lawn. She explained to him that they had an unfortunate divergence of opinion on this matter. While she felt called to do many things at that age, mowing the lawn was not one of them. In response, her father let her know that while he was interested in her opinion on many things, this was not one of them. And so, the next morning she found herself plodding around next to him: Learning how to turn the mower on and off using the pull string, when to empty the bag, and where to lug the clippings.

On her first day mowing, Rebekah felt the heat of the sun, the weight of the mower, and the weight of the injustice that her sisters didn't have to mow (she somehow glossed over the fact that she was several years older than them). Desperate to get fired, she did haphazard cuts all over the yard. She was sure when her dad got home he would be so stunned by her apparent incompetence, he would never ask her to mow again.

He found her that night after he got back from a long day at work and said, "Rebekah, I asked you to mow the lawn." She said, "I did." He said, "That's not what I call mowing." And she said, "Well, I did my best." Obviously, this was a bold-faced lie, but at this point she was committed to being deemed inept.

"Are you really telling me that I need to tell you what I do and don't mean when I ask you to mow the lawn?" her dad asked. She shook her head "no" and the next day went out and used the mower to carve her initials in the lawn.

Technically she had engaged in mowing of a sort, though this obviously fell in the category of "here's what I don't mean."

Now, in this situation, her dad probably didn't actually need to spell out that monogramming the yard wasn't what he meant when he asked her to mow the lawn. However, chore avoidance aside, "Here's what I don't mean" is a great strategy when you want someone to do or understand something new. We need to know the boundaries of a new idea in order to not overgeneralize when we are developing schemas, and we'll explore what this means and why it's so important in the rest of this chapter.

So, why do we even need non-examples? In large part, it's because humans aren't great at reasoning. We tend to make a lot of faulty generalizations. Here are a few examples.

Conversational Implicature

Cognitive psychologists (and most of us in human relationships) have found that one of the common ways we come to faulty conclusions is through the use of imprecise language. As we mentioned earlier, maybe Rebekah's dad shouldn't have had to say that cutting your initials into the yard doesn't count as cutting the grass. But technically, Rebekah *did* cut the grass because, without clarification of the boundaries, "cutting the grass" can mean a lot of different things.

Cognitive scientists call this idea – that our understanding of a word relies on our understanding of the conventions of communicative exchanges – conversational implicature. For example, if someone tells you their recipe for a batch of chocolate chip cookies calls for "some sugar and some salt" and you add a cup of salt and a teaspoon of sugar, technically you've added "some" of each, but the result won't taste very good.

It turns out we interpret imprecise terms like "some," which technically means "more than none," in context-specific ways. If we have the right background knowledge, we will know to interpret "some salt" and "some sugar" to mean very different amounts in a cookie recipe. Without that knowledge, we are lost.

Conversion Errors

Our trouble with ambiguous words like "some" doesn't stop here. Another common way we make faulty generalizations is by reversing terms we shouldn't like "some" and "all." These are called conversion errors. For example, the following are accurate statements:

> Some pies are desserts.
>
> Some desserts are pies.

Those of us who eat chicken pot pie know there are plenty of non-dessert pies, and this is an accurate statement. A conversion error, on the other hand, might sound like this:

> All cookies are desserts.
>
> All desserts are cookies.

Readers who love a good bowl of ice cream will obviously see the error with the second statement. The second statement should contain "some" instead of "all," but the speaker has assumed if the first is true, its inverse should be also.

The stakes of conversion errors are a lot higher when we move beyond the realm of desserts. Imagine the faulty decision making that could come from a conversion error like "All our top sellers this year were new hires. Therefore, all new hires will be top sellers." While this may sound glaringly wrong, unfortunately, errors like these are fairly common.

Using Non-Examples

Here's where non-examples come in. Non-examples bring clarity to a concept by making its boundaries bright. They keep us from over-generalizing and help build schemas more accurately and quickly.

You'll be happy to hear that not all of Rebekah's dad's attempts to teach her how to be helpful were as ill-fated as mowing. When he taught her to use a hammer, he modeled three different grips saying, "You aren't going to want to hold it too high, you won't have any leverage. If you hold it too low, you won't have any control. You want to hold it in this sweet spot in the middle, that way you'll have both power and precision."

We call this use of non-examples the Goldilocks effect. In the story of *Goldilocks and the Three Bears*, we might not know exactly what Goldi's "just right" porridge is, but we know it's somewhere between "too hot" and "too cold." In this case, Rebekah's dad could have told Rebekah where to hold the hammer. However, without the non-examples, she wouldn't have understood the rationale for where to hold it or the boundaries of the best grip. The maxim may be "Two wrongs don't make a right," but, in the case of building schemas, two wrongs get us a lot closer to what's right.

It's not just authors of fairy tales and Rebekah's dad who have caught on to this. Since the 1970s, cognitive scientists have found evidence that giving learners time to practice with both examples and non-examples facilitates faster and more robust concept development. They theorize this is because non-examples help learners understand the boundaries of the concept – by understanding what something isn't, learners more clearly understand what it is. Armed with that understanding, learners are less likely to make faulty generalizations.

For example, in 2008, Tsamir and other researchers were interested in how children developed their concept of triangles. They showed kindergarteners a variety of examples and non-examples of triangles. For each, they asked the children whether or not they were looking at a picture of a triangle and how they knew. They found that non-examples tended to work in two ways.

Some non-examples children could recognize as such immediately. For example, when researchers showed students a square, children said, "No!" They gave reasons like "It doesn't look like a triangle" or "That's a square."

Other non-examples were less intuitive and seemed to prompt a different type of reasoning. Students struggled to correctly categorize shapes the researchers called "almost triangles." For instance, when researchers showed students the shape below, only 5% could identify that it was not a triangle.

When students were asked about their incorrect answers, many referenced the figure's three-sidedness, suggesting they were tuning into some of its critical attributes (i.e. what makes a triangle a triangle). Children who answered correctly also referenced critical features, like the lack of three vertices, though they didn't use that terminology. Based on this work, the researchers found that non-examples that appear similar to examples on the surface (such as the "almost triangles") could be uniquely powerful for concept development when accompanied with dialogue to support learners in identifying the ways they do and don't align with critical features of the concept. Let's explore what this looks like in a generalizable mental model.

Here's What I Don't Mean in Practice

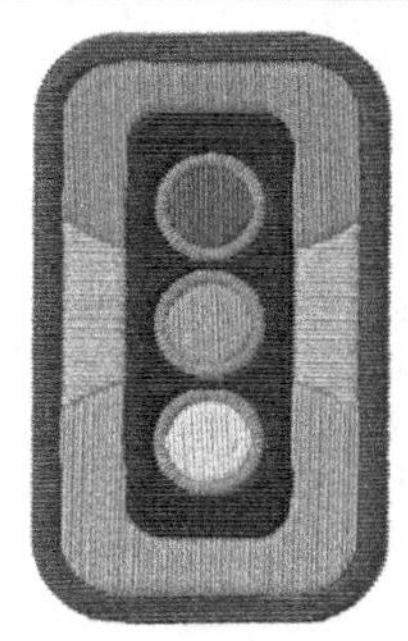

Big Idea: Use non-examples to provide boundaries to schemas.

Mental Model: Red Light, Green Light.

Ready to test out the use of non-examples? Let the title of the children's game Red Light, Green Light be your guide when you are introducing something new.

Imagine your organization wants to update the "careers" landing page on their website. You've tasked your team with drafting text for the new landing page and want to make sure they hit the right tone. Rather than just asking for a draft by next Tuesday, using the Red Light, Green Light approach, you might do something like this.

Step 1: Set It Up

Introduce the general idea or concept. For example, you might say something like "We want to communicate in a way that matches our brand. We're going for warm, trustworthy, and humble."

Step 2: Red Light, Green Light

First, give a non-example, preferably one that represents a likely mistake (think of the almost triangles). Then, pair that with an example.

Here, that might sound like "Here's an example and non-example of the brand-aligned text. I don't think the wording's quite right, but I wanted you to see what I do and don't mean by matching our brand's tone."

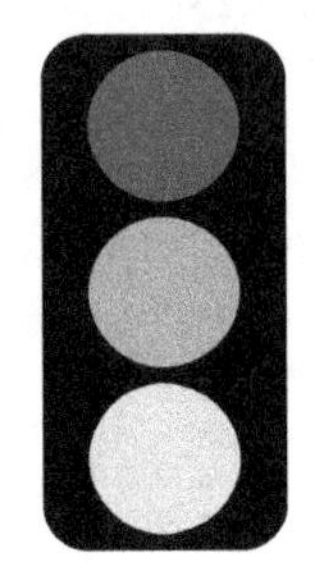	**Red Light:** Stuffy, impersonable, formal, unapproachable: "For decades our organization has taken a three-pronged approach to hiring. Each component holds expertise at the center."
	Green Light: Warm, inviting, trustworthy, humble: "We are always learning. Though our team has deep expertise, we view ourselves as lifelong students."

This could be helpful to your team for a few reasons. Remember conversational implicature? Telling someone to write in a tone that is "trustworthy" can be interpreted in a lot of different ways. When you provide an example coupled with a non-example, it's a lot easier for your team to see the boundaries of the tone and generate other examples of what this looks like independently.

Want to take it to the next level? Here are two suggestions.

- **Spotlight the critical features:** Explain *why* your non-example doesn't work to help others tune in to the boundaries of the concept. Remember the "almost triangles" and the suggestion that a teacher could support learning by explaining *why* a figure with rounded edges can't be a triangle? You can use similar explanations, or better yet, ask questions like "Why isn't X an example of Y?" to help others tune in to the critical features (e.g. "Given what you know about the three attributes of a triangle, why isn't this figure a triangle?"). In this case you might ask, "Why isn't saying 'For decades our organization has taken a three-pronged approach to hiring. Each component holds expertise at the center' aligned with our brand tone?"
- **Find the sweet spot:** If it works for the concept you want someone to learn, you can also provide two non-examples at opposite poles to show what the "just right" zone is in the middle.

In the case of updating the "careers" landing page, you've shown what stuffy looks like. Now tell them what you **don't** mean on the other end of the spectrum. You might give an example like "Hey you! Your dream position might be waiting." You can even couple this with a spotlight on the critical features saying something like "What would we have to change about this example to help it match our brand tone?"

When others have to identify that the non-example goes way beyond "warm" – it is so casual (not to mention corny) that it may undermine the credibility of your organization – they will know that you are asking them to find a sweet spot somewhere in between stuffy and casual. You help them identify the boundaries of your organizational tone, which will support them with this and future writing tasks.

Conclusion

Humans love to generalize. While in some cases this can be helpful, often it means people take what they hear and overstate the implications. Non-examples help counter this tendency. They provide boundaries to our schemas, which helps us apply what we learn accurately.

Takeaways

- Use non-examples to show what you **don't** mean or the boundaries of a concept. When you are learning something new, understanding what something isn't goes a long way in helping you understand what it is.
- Explain *why* your non-example doesn't work to help others identify the boundaries of the concept. Better yet, ask questions like "Why isn't X an example of Y?" to help others tune in to the critical features of a new idea.
- Look for opportunities to use two non-examples (e.g. too tall, too short) at opposite poles to show what the "just right" zone is in the middle.

References and further reading

Begg, I., & Harris, G. (1982). On the interpretation of syllogisms. *Journal of Verbal Learning and Verbal Behavior, 21*(5), 595–620.

Bills, L., Dreyfus, T., Mason, J., Tsamir, P., Watson, A., & Zaslavsky, O. (2006). Exemplification in mathematics education. In J. Novotná, H. Moraová, M. Krátká & N. Stehlíková (eds.) *Proceedings of the 30th Conference of the International Group for the Psychology of Mathematics Education Vol. 1*, pp. 126–154.

Dickstein, L. S. (1975). Effects of instructions and premise order on errors in syllogistic reasoning. *Journal of Experimental Psychology: Human Learning and Memory, 1*(4), 376–384.

Klausmeier, H. J., & Feldman, K. V. (1975). Effects of a definition and a varying number of examples and nonexamples on concept attainment. *Journal of Educational Psychology, 67*(2), 174–178.

McKinney, C. W., Larkins, A. G., Ford, M. J., & Davis III, J. C. (1983). The effectiveness of three methods of teaching social studies concepts to fourth-grade students: An aptitude-treatment interaction study. *American Educational Research Journal, 20*(4), 663–670.

Tsamir, P., Tirosh, D., & Levenson, E. (2008). Intuitive nonexamples: The case of triangles. *Educational Studies in Mathematics, 69*, 81–95.

PART 3

THE WHEELS OF COGNITION: ENCODING

In this section, we explore what has to happen if we want information to actually make it from working memory to long-term memory, and why it often doesn't make it back out again.

5. THE POWER OF WHY: DEEP PROCESSING VIA ELABORATIVE INTERROGATION

Jim's son Sam likes to play a game called *Why?*

The rules are simple: Sam begins by asking a question, and upon receiving the answer, he asks (you guessed it): "Why?" From here, he takes great delight in asking "why" of every subsequent response his father provides until Jim either runs out of patience or (more commonly) knowledge on the subject. Once the chain of whys hits the bedrock of Jim's understanding, so comes the sound of defeat as he is forced to say, "It... just *is*, okay!" at which point Sam takes delight in knowing that he has won another round of a game that is stacked significantly in his favor.

Despite this being an enjoyable game, at least for Sam, it hints at something more profound about the power of why. After all, our ability to ask that question is one of the most significant cognitive abilities we humans possess. We use it whenever we examine an idea, question a system, or look beyond the surface. Indeed, it's hard to imagine where we would be as a species were it not for our tendency to employ that word effectively.

But here's the thing. Not all whys are created equal. In fact, there are ways to ask why (or invite others to ask why) that are more effective than others. Thankfully, we have decades of research to help us understand (you guessed it) why this is the case, and it has something to do with what cognitive scientists call *elaborative interrogation*.

Let's start with the definition of each word. To *elaborate* is to add more to something and to *interrogate* is to question in ways that dig beneath the surface. Elaborative interrogation brings together these two concepts in ways that invite people to dig down and learn more.

But what does elaborative interrogation look like up close, and how can we use the power of why to our advantage?

The Science of Elaborative Interrogation

For the purposes of this chapter, we're going to explore two ways in which elaborative interrogation can be used to create better learning outcomes. We will refer to them as *depth* and *connection.*

Elaborative Interrogation and Depth

We know from research into how learning happens that there is a relationship between how deeply we think about something and the strength of the memory trace left behind by that thinking. When it comes to elaborative interrogation, we know that any question that invites someone to think deeply about an idea (often referred to by cognitive scientists as an "effortful" thought) will be more effective than one that does not. To illustrate what this might look like in practice, consider the following two questions and ask yourself why one is more likely to prompt deep processing than the other:

"In what year did Leo Szilard first develop his theory for nuclear chain reactions?"

"Why was the timing of Leo Szilard's discovery of nuclear chain reactions significant, given the year in which he made that breakthrough?"

As you can see, the first of these questions only requires shallow processing and there is little meaning attached to the answer. In this sense, the question could just as easily have been about the year Leo Szilard was born or the year he got married. The second question, on the other hand, attributes *significance* to the date. After all, the concept of chain reactions gave rise to the possibility of nuclear weapons, which ultimately changed the course of World War II and human history. This significance invites whoever is answering the question to attribute meaning to the year (it was 1933, by the way), which in turn makes it more memorable.

When this process of rich association happens at the level of words and language, researchers refer to it as *semantic involvement.* In one study, conducted in 1975 by Craik and Tulving, participants were shown a word on a screen for 20 milliseconds (essentially a flash) and then asked a question in relation to that word for which they had to respond "yes" or "no." After a short break, participants were given a surprise test to see how well they remembered the words on display. The researchers were able to influence how well participants remembered the words through the types of questions they asked. For instance, some were asked questions about whether the word rhymed with another word or whether it was written in upper or lower case. These surface-level questions prompted surface-level processing, which made those words less memorable. Conversely, when researchers followed the flashing word with a question that prompted participants to ascribe *meaning* to that word (e.g. the definition of the word), they were more likely to remember it in the test that followed.

Here's how this works. Experiments have shown that we remember more when retrieval cues match the encoding processes. For example, if we ask you to name the first letter of each word on a vocabulary list, unsurprisingly, you won't perform great on a memory test if the way we cue you to recall the words is to give you a list of synonyms. In our daily lives, most of what we have to do does *not* involve shallow processing (we aren't sure about you, but most of our work days are filled with tasks a bit more complex than "What's the first letter of this word?").

Cognitive scientists call this phenomenon the "transfer-appropriate processing perspective." According to this theory, deeper processing is associated with stronger recall because the meaning we make during deep processing is applicable across a wide range of retrieval contexts. Imagine that instead of asking you for the first letter of each word (shallow processing) we had asked you to use each word in a sentence (deep processing, focused on the *meaning* of the word). You would be able to use that information about the meaning of each word to complete a wide range of tasks, including defining the word, noting an antonym of the word as you read, and using it casually in conversation. Shallow processing, on the other hand, is only likely to support retrieval in very specific contexts (e.g. list words that start with 'B') that we rarely encounter in real life. We focus on deep processing because that's how most of us need to use information in our daily lives.

Elaborative Interrogation and Connection

In addition to inviting people to think deeply, we also know that inviting people to make connections is an effective way to support their development in a given domain. To explain why this is effective, consider the analogy of the burrs that latch onto your clothing (or your dog's fur) when going for a hike.

As you'll remember from chapter 3, a burr is remarkably good at hitching a ride on your dog's leg because of the many tiny hooks that cover its surface. The more hooks there are, the stickier the burr becomes. The same can be said of the information we present to people and the ways we can get people to think about that content through elaborative interrogation.

For example, consider the difference between these two questions:

"Does a dolphin breathe using gills or lungs?"

"Why isn't a dolphin a fish?"

Answering the first question comes in the form of a choice between gills and lungs. The second question, on the other hand, requires you to consider a) what makes a fish a fish and b) whether a dolphin meets those criteria. To extend our analogy, this second question is a stickier "burr" because there are more informational "hooks." To answer, you could talk about how dolphins are warm- rather than cold-blooded, how they have to surface for air, or how they give birth to live young rather than lay eggs.

Each of these responses offers a potential connection between what the person already knows (like specific characteristics of fish versus mammals) and what you want them to understand (why they should classify a dolphin as a mammal, not a fish). There are many ways to achieve this, and we will continue to explore the idea of prior knowledge in the next chapter. For now, it's important to know that elaborative interrogation helps people to integrate new information into their existing understanding, and "hooking" it to what they already know makes it more likely they will remember the information later.

For example, in one study conducted in 1987 by Michael Pressley and a team of researchers, participants were shown a series of sentences describing the actions of a man. In one group, both his actions and his rationale were included in the same statement ("The hungry man got into the car to go to the restaurant"). Another group was instead prompted with an elaborative question to offer their own rationale ("Why did that particular man do that?"), while a third group was simply given the basic core of the sentence ("The hungry man got into the car"). When participants were later asked to recall details from the sentences, the group that had been invited to elaborate by considering why the man had engaged in the action significantly outperformed the other two groups at remembering the details in question. Active processing that required participants to connect what they already know ("I go to restaurants when I am hungry") and new information (the sentence they are reading about a man getting into a car) made it more memorable.

Experimental studies have revealed that elaborative interrogation is most effective at inviting such connections when they are precise rather than vague, and when there is a higher degree of prior knowledge on the part of the learner. For instance, in a 1992 study led by Vera Woloshyn, researchers presented Canadian and German students with geographical facts about the two countries. This meant each group had higher prior knowledge in one case (their home country) than the other. In cases where prior knowledge was higher, the impact of elaborative interrogation on learning was higher. This is consistent with the point about "connection" earlier. Learners with higher background knowledge had more facts in long-term memory to which they could hook the new information.

So, we now know that when people process information with depth and connection, they are more likely to remember it. How might we go about crafting such questions and how can we use them to our advantage? For that, we will turn to our next mental model.

The Power of Why in Practice

Big Idea: When learners process ideas with depth and connection, that information is more likely to stick, so we should ask questions that invite elaborative interrogation.

Mental Model: The Archeological Dig.

Archeology Tip 1: Dig Deeper, Learn More

If you found yourself on an archeological dig and came across a shiny object sticking out of the ground, it's unlikely that you would just brush off some surrounding debris, marvel at what you have seen, and walk away. You would keep digging until you were able to uncover the entire object. We need learners to similarly dig deeper, instead of being satisfied with surface understanding. We know by now that this is because inviting people to interrogate ideas beyond their surface features is a powerful way to foster growth and retention.

Questions that help you prompt for depth include:

- **"How do you know?"** (e.g. "You said it's accelerating. How do you know?").
- **"Explain this process to me. How does this work?"** (e.g. "Explain the process of calculating gross margin to me. How does it work?").
- Sam's favorite question, **"Why?"** (e.g. "Why do you think I want to start by targeting clients in the southeast?").

Each of these questions prompts the respondent to keep digging beyond the surface to elaborate on their original answer. As we've discussed, the work the learner has to do to answer these questions adds more detail to their schema and makes it more likely they'll remember the information later.

Here's what digging deeper can look like in the real world. Imagine your team, which has no background in project management, needs to plan an upcoming project and present their plan for approval. You could give a presentation on the basics of project management, but your team will be more likely to remember the information if you prompt them to engage in deep processing about each key idea. For example, after introducing the template they'll use to define roles and responsibilities on the project, you might ask questions like:

- "Let's do a quick recap. How did we define roles and responsibilities? What were the four steps we used and why does each matter?"
- "It may seem like extra work, but why do you think I am asking you to list the percentage of time each team member is actually available in addition to the percentage of time they are needed on the project?"

It's worth the time to prompt them to dig deeper because you avoid "in one ear, out the other" syndrome. The team will be more likely to retain the process for defining roles and responsibilities in the future if they've had to articulate *how* to do it and *why* it matters.

Archeology Tip 2: Dig Smarter, Learn More

Archeologists are a careful bunch. When they find something of value, they will handle it delicately and document their findings in very specific ways. For instance, rather than simply labeling an item "mirror," they would be more likely to tag it as "a silver mirror, engraved with a geometric design, probably made for a child." They do this because they know that organizing items in this way is crucial if you want other researchers to identify and make sense of the artifact by its constituent parts (child, silver, engraved) and connect it to their own work.

Our minds operate in similar ways whenever we are committing things to long-term memory. Just like in our "burr" example earlier, the more tags or hooks a piece of information has, the sticker it becomes and the more opportunities we have to make sense of it and access it at a later date. We know that elaborative interrogation can prompt people to make more of these critical connections.

An example of an elaborative question that prompts connections would be "What would happen if I changed X to Y?" This invites the respondent to explore their underlying characteristics of two different ideas and draw connections between them (e.g. asking a third-grader, "We know that 5 + 2 = 7, but what would happen if I changed the plus sign to a multiplication sign?"). You could also ask, "Why would this be true of X but not Y?" This question explores differences, which will prompt the learner to draw key distinctions (e.g. asking an aspiring lawyer, "Why would this be true of a federal crime but not a state crime?"). "How are they related?" is another easy way to get people to articulate important connections.

If you were trying to help your team dig smarter while they learn the basics of project management, you could use questions that help them integrate knowledge, including:

- "We've talked about the core tenets of a successful project. On time, on target, and on budget. How are the team's actions related to each tenet?"
- "Let's spell out the relationship between these tenets for a second. What will happen to the budget if our timeline is fixed and scope increases? Alternatively, what are our options if we have a project underway and we have to cut the budget?"
- "Why will the timeline for this project be higher priority than it was for the last one you worked on?"

Conclusion

Ideas are complex things possessing near-limitless dimensions, many of which we never get to see. As such, there are many ways to think about an idea, but not all are conducive to learning. The questions we ask can often prove to be the difference between misguided, surface-level thinking and learning that is deep, nuanced, and durable. Whenever we prompt someone to dig deeper, and draw more connections to a new idea, we reveal more of its inherent fullness and increase the likelihood that it will be remembered. Elaborative interrogation offers us a means for opening up that richness and inviting others to do the same.

Takeaways

- Cognitive science tells us that when we think about an idea with depth and connection, we will be more likely to remember it and use that idea again in the future.
- To help people process information and preserve memory traces, we can employ elaborative interrogation.
- Among other characteristics, elaborative interrogation invites people to think beyond the surface features of an idea, to offer justifications or rationale for the conclusions they draw, and to make connections between what they already know and are coming to understand.

References and further reading

Bransford, J. D., Franks, J. J., Morris, C.D., & Stein, B.S. (1979). Some general constraints on learning and memory research. In L. S. Cermak & F. I. M. Craik (eds.) *Levels of Processing in Human Memory.* Hillsdale, NJ: Lawrence Erlbaum Associates Inc., pp. 331–354.

Craik, F. I. M., & Lockhart, R. S. (1972). Levels of processing: A framework for memory research. *Journal of Verbal Learning and Verbal Behavior, 11*(6), 671–684.

Craik, F. I. M., & Tulving, E. (1975). Depth of processing and the retention of words in episodic memory. *Journal of Experimental Psychology: General, 104*(3), 268–294.

Dunlosky, J., Rawson, K. A., Marsh, E. J., Nathan, M. J., & Willingham, D. T. (2013). Improving students' learning with effective learning techniques: Promising directions from cognitive and educational psychology. *Psychological Science in the Public Interest, 14*(1), 4–58.

Pressley, M., McDaniel, M. A., Turnure, J. E., Wood, E., & Ahmad, M. (1987). Generation and precision of elaboration: Effects on intentional and incidental learning. *Journal of Experimental Psychology: Learning, Memory, and Cognition, 13*(2), 291–300.

Pressley, M., Symons, S., McDaniel, M. A., Snyder, B. L., & Turnure, J. E. (1988). Elaborative interrogation facilitates acquisition of confusing facts. *Journal of Educational Psychology, 80*(3), 268–278.

Shondrick, S. J., Dinh, J. E., & Lord, R. G. (2010). Developments in implicit leadership theory and cognitive science: Applications to improving measurement and understanding alternatives to hierarchical leadership. *The Leadership Quarterly, 21*(6), 959–978.

Willingham, D. T., & Riener, C. (2019). *Cognition: The Thinking Animal.* Cambridge: Cambridge University Press.

Woloshyn, V. E., Pressley, M., & Schneider, W. (1992). Elaborative-interrogation and prior-knowledge effects on learning of facts. *Journal of Educational Psychology, 84*(1), 115–124.

6. CLIMB HIGHER: ACTIVATING PRIOR KNOWLEDGE

"I send greetings on behalf of the people of our planet. We step out of our solar system into the universe seeking only peace and friendship, to teach if we are called upon, to be taught if we are fortunate." These words, uttered by then Secretary-General of the United Nations Kurt Waldheim, are the first to appear on what is perhaps the most ambitious and hopeful act of communication in human history: Two gold-coated copper phonograph records, affixed to the twin Voyager probes launched on August 20th and September 5th 1977, with the express aim of transmitting to extraterrestrials a snapshot of life on Earth.

In their book *Murmurs of Earth*, astrophysicist Carl Sagan and his team of collaborators recount the monumental task of curating a representative slice of humankind for the viewing and listening pleasure of alien life. Sagan describes how, after an exhaustive process, the team settled on a collection of greetings in 55 ancient and modern languages, a variety of natural Earth sounds, 90 minutes of music, and 115 photographs from around the globe. Among them, one can find everything from the structure of DNA, to the calling of humpback whales, to Chuck Berry's 1958 rock 'n' roll classic "Johnny B. Goode."

Just as important as determining *what* would go into this depiction of life on Earth was the question of *how* such information might be interpreted by forms of life entirely unlike our own – a fact not lost on another of the compilers, the artist Jon Lomberg, who noted: "I would look at pictures and try to imagine that I'd never seen the subject before. How could the photograph be misinterpreted? What was ambiguous?"

The team knew that any predictions as to the meaning extraterrestrials might make of these artifacts were essentially acts of guesswork. For them, nested within the unlikely event of Voyager's message ever being received was the even less likely event that the recipients would understand it. After all, as Lomberg posited, it could be that these forms of life "have no senses as we understand them."

In essence, Sagan and Lomberg were wrestling with an extraterrestrial extension of a reality cognitive scientists have known for a generation: *We come to understand new information in reference to what we already know. As such, we need to consider how prior knowledge is activated whenever we encounter something new to be learned.* Thankfully, understanding the role that prior knowledge plays in learning is a little easier to do here on Earth, but it's still a process that requires us to appreciate how our minds encounter and organize information.

Why Prior Knowledge Matters

Those behind the Voyager gold disc project lived more in hope than reality because of the fact that any new idea must rely on existing knowledge as its frame of reference. In their case, there was no picture of prior extraterrestrial knowledge from which to draw. But this only helps to tell us one part of the "prior knowledge" story. For the rest, we must return to some of our foundational cognitive science principles.

At the outset of the book, we explored a "simple model of the mind," which describes the relationship between our environment, the attention we pay to it, and our short- and long-term memory; in chapter 2 we introduced the idea of schemas, which we defined as connected networks of concepts. Well, it turns out that there is a connection between these two models that explains why it's important to consider prior knowledge as a crucial part of learning. Whenever we confront an idea, certain knowledge items (or nodes) are activated within our prior knowledge (or schemas). These nodes are best defined as those concepts our long-term memory considers relevant to the information we are encountering.

For instance, saying the word "car" activates in the long-term memory of the listener a whole host of connected terms and images associated with that concept. From there, one can activate additional nodes by offering additional variations on the idea. Adding a qualifier like "sports car" (fast, dangerous, high-performing) as opposed to "family car" (reliable, sturdy, unglamorous) activates ever more nuanced schemas in our long-term memory, such that "car" can become many things to us at once. Now imagine you've gone back in time and were trying to describe the phrase "electric car" to someone from the 1870s. You would have to contend with how to describe an entirely novel concept, with little to no natural points of connection to prior knowledge.

Another way to understand the importance of prior knowledge, or the absence of it, is to experience it for yourself. Take a look at the following excerpt and ask yourself: Expressed as a percentage, how much of this text would I be able to recall if I was tested on it at the end of reading this chapter?

> The Black Caps slipped from 109 for one to 110 for four when Rachin Ravindra fell for 32, Will Young for 54 and Daryl Mitchell for one, but skipper Tom Latham and man-of-the-match Glenn Phillips led their fightback. The pair put on 144 for the fifth wicket in just under 26 overs before Phillips was caught by Rashid Khan off Naveen-ul-Haq. That left New Zealand on 254 for five and Mark Chapman's quickfire 25 off 12 lifted them to 288.

If your answer is less than 5%, you are not alone. Or at least you are not alone in the United States. If you grew up in another country such as England, Australia, or India, then it's likely that your recall percentage would be higher. The reason? The excerpt is from a report on a cricket match, which is far from familiar to many in the United States.

The important thing to name here is that the language itself is straightforward. Any literate adult would understand the words on the page. The differentiating factor, therefore, is not whether you understand the individual words but whether you have the required background knowledge to understand the broader meaning of what is being conveyed. It's this prior knowledge that plays the biggest part in whether you will understand and recall the cricket report.

Research has repeatedly shown that prior knowledge plays an important part in memory and learning. In one classic 1972 study by Bransford and Johnson, researchers used a similar approach to the earlier example, by handing participants a cryptic text that would be difficult to decipher unless the person knew the topic upon which it was based. The researchers then split participants into two groups, providing one with the topic behind the text and leaving the other group unaware. At a later date, the two groups were asked to recall as much information from the text as they could. Sure enough, the group who knew the topic upon which it was based (and who therefore could rely on prior knowledge of that topic) were able to recall more parts of the text than those who did not

The prevailing theory for why comes back to our model of the mind. When we encounter a concept, prior knowledge helps guide us to those details that are most worthy of attention, meaning we don't waste precious working memory on the less important parts. Prior knowledge also provides a pre-existing network of ideas (or schema) into which the new knowledge can be assimilated. In this regard, you can think of schemas for a given idea as a giant jigsaw puzzle, and any new idea as a jigsaw piece that we can either add to an ever-evolving picture of the idea at hand, or not.

In cases when there is no prior knowledge, or indeed whenever prior knowledge isn't activated, there is no larger picture into which the new puzzle piece can fit. Without a schematic place to call home, the new idea is much less likely to be encoded into our long-term memory, and even if some trace of the memory remains, its dislocated status will make it much more difficult to access. In other words, new ideas need to establish a connection to our existing schemas, otherwise they are unlikely to stick and we won't be able to call upon them in the future.

Why the Right Kind of Prior Knowledge Matters

In addition to the existence of prior knowledge, the accuracy and relevance of that prior knowledge also matters for learning. Indeed, researchers have shown how having inaccurate or incomplete prior knowledge can be even more of a hindrance to learning than having no prior knowledge at all, thus giving scientific credence to the old saying "A little knowledge can be a dangerous thing." To extend our jigsaw puzzle analogy, this would be like trying to connect new knowledge pieces to the larger puzzle of our prior knowledge, but the pieces don't quite fit together because some are from the wrong puzzle.

Prominent examples of faulty connections between prior and new knowledge are common (but by no means exclusive) in young children. In one recent example from our own lives, Jim's 4-year-old daughter Nora pointed to a helicopter in a picture book and referred to it as an airplane. This misappropriation of two similar but non-identical concepts is understandable for a child of that age, but it also shows how humans spend most of their time connecting new information to prior knowledge with varying degrees of success. If such errors were never rectified, that faulty prior knowledge could play a detrimental part in future learning, like a bug in a computer system that stands to corrupt the future uploading of new information.

Indeed, there are predictable pitfalls one can fall into when activating prior knowledge that it pays to avoid. These include:

- **Completely irrelevant prior knowledge:** This is when you invite people to pull details from their long-term memories that have nothing to do with the new information you want them to understand. For example, imagine leading a group of newly promoted managers through a session on the basics of budget management at your organization. When you highlight that they'll need to plan for both variable expenses and fixed costs, you'll want them to understand that a fixed cost is a budget item that typically doesn't change from month to month or quarter to quarter (e.g. employee salaries), whereas a variable expense is a cost that can change over time (e.g. cost of materials). Imagine that upon seeing the words "fixed" and "variable" on a slide, a trainee starts thinking, "Ah, I know what you mean by 'fixed'. I recently fixed several things in my apartment. Replacing the drywall doesn't come cheap." In this case, you would have succeeded in activating prior knowledge, but that knowledge is entirely irrelevant to the task at hand or the knowledge you're hoping to build towards.

- **Partially relevant prior knowledge:** We tend to refer to this as "knowing just enough to be dangerous," and it often comes with that most unfortunate of traits: The illusion of understanding. Continuing our variable expenses vs. fixed expenses example, imagine if the trainee said, "Ah, I know expenses. I filled out expense forms at my previous organization. That was how we would get reimbursed for travel." Now, the invocation of "expenses" in this case is a little closer to its intended meaning within this context, but the application of the term is still underdeveloped and inaccurate (after all, not all expenses are created equal, which is the whole point of differentiating between variable and fixed). In cases such as these, doing nothing will result in new knowledge being built upon faulty assumptions, which often leads to confusion down the line.
- **Relevant prior knowledge that the learner doesn't realize is relevant:** We think of this as knowledge that *would* be useful if activated but which remains dormant or "hiding in plain sight." Extending our example about fixed vs. variable costs, imagine one of your trainees worked in an ice cream store as a teenager. Moreover, imagine that the trainee regularly heard their boss talk about how his rent for the building stayed the same but the cost of ice cream and other ingredients would vary from month to month, depending on the time of year. A case like this is the equivalent of an open goal in terms of the relevant prior knowledge. However, if that learner isn't supported in connecting their relevant prior knowledge to what you want them to understand (i.e. the ways in which it's a perfect example of variable expenses vs. fixed costs) then that connection is likely to remain unrealized and the new information is likely to be forgotten.

As you can see, more than serving simply as a frame of reference, our existing knowledge provides us with a jumping-off point from which to branch out and connect to new information that would otherwise be beyond our reach, as long as we go about making that connection with intentionality. Given this tendency, the challenge becomes one of inviting learners to draw on the relevant parts of their existing knowledge so that they can make the most meaningful connections to the new idea.

Activating Prior Knowledge in Practice

Big Idea: We come to understand new information by reference to our existing knowledge and, as such, we need to consider how prior knowledge is activated whenever we encounter something new to be learned.

Mental Model: The Rock Climber.

Consider the analogy of rock climbing. When scaling a rock face, climbers rely on footholds and handholds. In order to progress, the climber first identifies a point in the rock to establish a foothold before using their legs to drive their body upwards and secure a new handhold. You can think of prior knowledge as a foothold (the established, secure understanding of an existing idea) and new knowledge a handhold (the as yet unattained concept that we stretch out and hope to secure).

Just like rock climbing, the connections between the footholds of prior knowledge and the handholds of new understanding are not always secure, and unless we're intentional about shoring up such connections, there's a good chance that any potential new learning will simply fall away.

To underscore, the key for ensuring strong connections between prior knowledge and new understanding resides in the efficacy and accuracy with which we *activate* that prior knowledge – but what does this look like in practice, and how can we use prior knowledge activation to bring about more effective learning?

To illustrate what prior knowledge activation looks like in everyday life, imagine your young nephew has been struggling at school. While you are visiting, your brother mentions math homework has become a particular source of tension between them and asks if you would be willing to work with your nephew. He doesn't understand the basic principles of division but doesn't want help from his parents.

Here's how you could use the principles of the "rock climber" to activate your nephew's prior knowledge in order to help him better understand division.

The Handhold: Where Do You Want the Learner to Go?

Decide on the deep structure of the idea you want to convey. First of all, you need to answer a simple but deceptively tricky question: What *precisely* is the information I want my learner to take from this experience? This will be the destination you want them to reach by means of their existing knowledge. The "deep structure" part refers to the specific internal architecture of the idea rather than surface features that don't tell the full story – like mistakenly assuming that a helicopter is the same as an airplane just because they both fly. Precision is therefore important since any lack of clarity at this stage could lead to you targeting the wrong content and activating unhelpful prior knowledge.

In the case of your nephew, you could articulate the idea you want to convey as follows:

> **The Handhold: Where do you want the learner to go?**
>
> I want him to understand that division is the equal distribution of a quantity.

The Foothold: Where is the Learner Starting from?

Determine what relevant prior knowledge the learner has at their disposal. If meaningful access to new knowledge is determined by what we already know, then identifying any relevant prior knowledge the learner might hold is a critical next step. It might not be immediately clear (to you or the learner) which parts of their existing knowledge are pertinent to understanding the new idea, so come to the learner where they are at and try to be cognizant of any *relevant* prior knowledge that could be hiding in plain sight.

Here that might be:

The Foothold: Where is the learner starting from?

My nephew and I love to play card games, and he always asks to be the dealer.

The Climb: How Can You Bridge the Gap between the Two?

Introduce the new idea via the existing knowledge and make that connection explicit. This is where you draw on what the learner already knows as the framing for what you want them to know. Before engaging in this step, it's important to double-check that you're not dealing in vaguely connected analogies (e.g. riding a bicycle is *somewhat* similar to driving a car but knowing how to do the former does not provide us with everything we need to do the latter).

Instead you need to identify and match concepts that share the same underlying structure as one another, even though they might appear different on the surface. Once you're clear on the connection, the key is now to make the connection between what they know and what you want them to understand unambiguously clear.

Here, this might involve making the following connections between prior knowledge and new understanding extremely explicit. For instance:

The Climb: How can you bridge the gap between the two?

- Give your nephew 12 cards and invite him to deal them out to four imagined player so that each gets the same number.
- Say: "Whenever you deal a set of cards and ensure each player gets the same amount, you are in fact doing a form of division. That's because division happens when we equally distribute a total into equal shares. Let's look at how we could write what you just did as an equation: $12 \div 4 = 3$."
- Say: "When you think about what you did with the cards, what does each number and symbol in the equation represent? What do you think will happen to the equation if we changed the total number of cards to 16? Why?"

Conclusion

Perhaps the simplest question we can ask whenever we introduce someone to a new idea is "Are they picking up what I'm putting down?" Whether you're dealing with extraterrestrial forms of life or plain old humans, one way to be more certain that real learning is taking place is to ask a second, more instructive question: "What do they already know that will enable them to pick up what I'm putting down?"

In this regard, prior knowledge is a vital but often overlooked component of how we learn and develop. Remember, this is not simply a case of relying on surface-level comparisons between people's prior knowledge and the content you want them to remember. Vague analogies and lazy similes are just that, and telling someone that assembling a dresser is just like completing a jigsaw puzzle will only lead to faulty connections and incomplete understanding of irrelevant knowledge.

Instead, we need to decide on the deep structure of the idea we want to convey, identify what the learner is bringing to the table, then match what is already known to what we want them to learn in an authentic, generative way. In doing so, we provide the best chance of building durable knowledge from existing understanding.

Takeaways

- All new information must be assimilated into our existing schemas in order for us to organize and recall it.
- The manner in which we assimilate that information (i.e. the degree of relevant connection between our prior knowledge and the new idea) impacts both the likelihood of that information being stored in long-term memory for future use, and whether the information being encoded is accurate and complete.
- When we make such connections explicit, learners better understand how "what I already know" fits into "what I'm coming to know."

References and further reading

Bransford, J. D., & Johnson, M. K. (1972). Contextual prerequisites for understanding: Some investigations of comprehension and recall. *Journal of Verbal Learning and Verbal Behavior, 11*(6), 717–726.

Craik, F. I. M., & Lockhart, R. S. (1972). Levels of processing: A framework for memory research. *Journal of Verbal Learning and Verbal Behavior, 11*(6), 671–684.

Ferris, T. (2017). *How the Voyager Golden Record Was Made.* The New Yorker. Available at: www.newyorker.com/tech/annals-of-technology/voyager-golden-record-40th-anniversary-timothy-ferris (Accessed: 29 November 2024).

Lipson, M. Y. (1982). Learning information from text: The role of prior knowledge and reading ability. *Journal of Reading Behavior, 14*(3), 243–261.

Sagan, C., et al. (1978). *Murmurs of Earth.* London: Ballantine Books.

Shing, Y. L., & Brod, G. (2016). Effects of prior knowledge on memory: Implications for education. *Mind, Brain, and Education, 10*(3), 153–161.

Willingham D. T., & Riener, C. (2019). *Cognition: The Thinking Animal* (4th ed.). Cambridge: Cambridge University Press.

7. WHAT'S THE STORY?: THE POWER OF NARRATIVES

"It was a cold night in the forest, and I was starting to grow tired. Stumbling into a clearing I saw a light on a hill, then chimney smoke, and the faint outline of a small cottage. Drawing closer still, I was met with a strange sight: A batch of birchwood brooms with gnarled wooden handles stacked against the cottage wall. I knocked, and the door heaved open to reveal a tall woman made taller by her pitch-black, pointy hat. It was then that it dawned on me: I was standing face-to-face with a..."

Now, how is it that you knew what the next word of the story would be? What was it about your experience of stories that enabled you to arrive at that word? Convention, expectation, and background knowledge allowed you to name it, and the way the story was shaped led you unequivocally to that point.

Narratives are powerful since they both shape and reflect our experience of the world. What's more, we have come to understand that the traditional conventions of narrative (be that tropes like the example above or recognizable narrative structures) possess characteristics that make them uniquely memorable. But what is it about stories that make them more accessible, consumable, and memorable, and how might we harness that power to communicate more effectively?

Why Narratives Matter

Well-crafted stories are a mode of information sharing that humans find easier to remember than if that same information was presented in a non-narrative form. Cognitive scientists use the term *narrativity* to describe the extent to which information is story-like in its presentation. It's a relatively straightforward concept to illustrate. Consider the following two excerpts on the subject of chemistry and ask yourself, "If I wanted to remember the key details of this passage, which of the two would be more likely to stick and why?"

- **Option 1:** The radioactive elements in pitchblende rock are powerful enough to withstand most acids, even at the highest temperatures. However, nonradioactive elements like iron, carbon, and uranium will react with different types of acids and either turn into a gas and dissolve away or turn into whole solid clumps. On the other hand, radioactive elements will remain unchanged.
- **Option 2:** Like true chemists, Marie and Pierre burned the pitchblende at different temperatures and added different kinds of acid to see what would happen. If they burned the rock too quickly or added too much acid, all of the pitchblende would be gone or destroyed, and they would have to start all over again. Marie learned from their experiments that the radioactivity stayed even after many other elements were burned away. She also learned that the radioactivity would not react with most acids. Even when she and Pierre added different acids to the pitchblende, the radioactivity was unchanged. The nonradioactive elements, like iron and carbon, would react with acid and either turn into a gas and dissolve away or turn into whole solid clumps, which could be removed from the pitchblende.

In one 1975 study into the organization of prose and its effects on memory, Bonnie Meyer and researchers measured participants' comprehension and memory of the information in these two texts immediately after reading and once again a week after reading. It turned out that option 2 (the high-narrativity version) was significantly easier for readers to remember than option 1 (the low-narrativity version).

There are a few theories as to why high-narrativity information is easier to comprehend and remember. Many of these have to do with attention, depth of processing, and prior knowledge, all of which we have discussed in previous chapters. Well, it turns out that stories with high levels of narrativity add another dimension to the mix, something researchers call *causal coherence*. Causal coherence theory basically states that when we encounter a text or story, we don't just remember the ideas and events explicitly presented. We also remember the relationships between the ideas and events being presented.

Even more intriguing is that there appears to be a sweet spot of causal coherence that makes things particularly memorable, which we can again explore through a straightforward set of examples. Consider the following sentences and again ask yourself which you think best lends itself to being remembered by the listener:

- **Option 1:** I bit into a slice of pizza that was still hot from the oven and ended up burning the roof of my mouth.
- **Option 2:** I ordered a pizza and ended up burning the roof of my mouth.
- **Option 3:** I went out for the day and ended up burning the roof of my mouth.

We probably all agree that option 3 is the hardest to access and remember because there isn't a clear connection between events (how does going out relate to a burned mouth?). You might also take issue with option 1 because the connection between the events is undermined by the unnecessary length and level of detail. Indeed, researchers have been able to demonstrate that option 2 is the easiest to remember because it achieves the sweet spot of causal connection: Not too obvious like option 1, and not too obscure like option 3. Indeed, option 2 works best because the listener is invited to *make an inference* between the cause (a pizza order) and the effect (a burned mouth). But how does this work? What is it about having to make an inference that makes a piece of information more memorable?

As we know from chapter 5 on elaborative interrogation, in order to remember something we first need to pay attention to it, and the more deeply we think about something, the more likely we are to be able to encode it into our long-term memory. In the case of causal coherence, inferring the meaning causes us to consider the piece of information more closely and effortfully. It is as though the sentence leaves a gap between the pizza and the burned mouth, a missing puzzle piece that we must work to identify so that we can fill in the causal relationship between the two. It might seem overly simple to infer that *the person must have bitten into the pizza*, but making that connection only becomes possible if we pay close attention to the corresponding parts of the sentence – and it is precisely the quality of that attention that makes it more memorable.

Another way of thinking about the sweet spot of causal coherence is to consider what makes a joke funny. Make a joke too obvious and it will likely elicit a groan; make the joke too obscure and you'll fall into the old adage "If you have to explain it then it's not funny." In fact, what makes for a good joke is the established tension between the set-up and punchline, and like effective causal coherence, the listener has to *do some work* to fill the meaning in the middle.

Like any good joke, good stories focus our attention on the parts that matter by presenting them in recognizably connected ways, while still leaving enough work to be done to engage us in each to-be-remembered moment.

Archetypal Narrative Structures and Memory

The scary story trope at the outset of this chapter illustrates another evidence-based theory about narrative structures and their usefulness. Research into the relationship between narrative and memory has shown that the more people know about textual and/or narrative structures, the better able they are to both comprehend and recall the information found within those stories and texts.

In other words, we use our understanding and expectations of narrative structures to guide our understanding and aid our recall of them – a phenomenon that can play out in the following ways: 1) by utilizing typical narrative structures, and 2) by referencing well-known stories.

Utilizing Typical Narrative Structures

Much has been written about typical narrative structures and the finite number of plots that inform the way we tell and hear stories. This idea that stories tend to fall into a number of predictable structures has been drawn upon by researchers as they explore whether some structures are more memorable than others.

For instance, studies have shown that texts or narratives with *chronological* narrative structures are easier to remember than stories in which chronology plays no part. Even more than chronology, researchers have shown how *problem-response* narrative structures (in which a complication is presented and then resolved) result in better comprehension and memory of the narrative or text in question.

A good example of this is the classic murder-mystery structure in which we are provided with a "set-up" (an established setting where everything appears normal); a "complication" (the murder); and the gradual move towards a resolution (the arrival of a detective and the solving of the crime). Indeed, the more one looks, the easier it is to see that problem-response narratives exist everywhere: So much so that it's hard to think of a story in which the introduction of a problem and its subsequent resolution *doesn't* play a part.

So, murder mysteries rely on a highly recognizable problem-response structure. Similar to the case of causal coherence, researchers have postulated that the reason the problem-response structure aids memory is because the audience is, once again, "put to work." In murder mysteries, readers have to apply their background knowledge to try to solve the mystery before the detective does.

We also know from research that archetypal narrative structures can be used to lighten the cognitive load of the listener or viewer. Since we know that attention is a finite resource and we can't possibly attend to everything, such archetypes can be powerful because they tell us where to direct our gaze. For example, in a murder mystery, we know we ought to pay close attention to the set-up, since those details will be operative in solving the murder. That is to say, if someone recognizes the narrative structure, they will know what is worth paying more attention to versus other story elements that might be less important.

The takeaway? Use narrativity to your advantage. If you want people to attend to and remember what you have to say, present it as a story and be intentional about the narrative structure you wish to employ.

Referencing Well-Known Stories

In addition to utilizing typical narrative structures, researchers have demonstrated how we are more inclined to pay careful attention to stories that make "call backs" to pre-existing stories and well-known narratives. In one ingenious study conducted in 2004 by Chen, Mo, and Honomichl, two groups of students were asked to solve the following problem:

> A treasure hunter is going to explore a cave on a hill near a beach. He suspected there might be many paths inside the cave so he was afraid he might get lost. Obviously, he did not have a map of the cave; all that he had with him were some common items such as a flashlight and a bag. What could he do to make sure he did not get lost trying to get out of the cave later?

When American college students were presented with this problem, 75% offered the correct answer: The treasure hunter should use pebbles from the beach to mark out his path into the cave and retrace his steps. Comparatively, when Chinese college students were presented with the same problem, only 25% of them answered it correctly.

The reason? Researchers designed the problem as a riff on the *Hansel and Gretel* fairy tale, which is well-known across the US but not well-known at all in China. When researchers switched the problem to map onto a well-known Chinese story instead, the trend in correct response rates reversed. In essence, researchers were able to show how references to recognizable narratives offered a roadmap for the respondent, inviting them to pay attention to the significant, operative parts of the problem. All of which brings us to our next mental model.

Narrativity in Practice

Big Idea: People pay better attention to and remember more from stories, so we should present information utilizing high-narrativity structures.

Mental Model: The Goldilocks Principle.

Draw on what you know about storytelling to convey information in ways that are "just right."

Imagine you've been put in charge of an internship initiative at your organization that offers on-the-job work experience to college-age students from the local community. You quickly notice something: Despite your organization being situated in a racially and socioeconomically diverse community, prior cohorts of the internship initiative have not reflected that diversity.

As you dig further, you find that attracting and recruiting a cohort of interns representative of the local area is in fact one of the stated aims of the initiative. You seek out your predecessor, who informs you that she would present application data indicating this lack of representation to the leadership team at the end of each recruitment cycle but that nothing was done to address or even acknowledge the matter. She shares how "It was as though they would forget about the message I was trying to convey before I had even left the room."

If your aim was to deliver a presentation that summarizes the recruitment shortcomings – and do so in such a way that is memorable so that it's more likely to lead to the changes you hope to see – how might you utilize narrativity to do so?

Step 1: Be Intentional about the Narrative Structure You Intend to Employ

If you want to make your argument impactful and memorable then it pays to reference specific narratives you know your audience will recognize (remember how researchers used *Hansel and Gretel*?) or draw on well-established narrative structures to inform how you communicate your message. These will, in turn, increase the narrativity of your presentation, which we know to be more effective at garnering memorable attention. Here is a list of archetypal narrative structures that can be utilized to make more memorable the information you are hoping to convey.

Narrative Structure	Definition
Definition/description	Explores the characteristic features of something.
Chronological	Presents events in the order in which they happened.
Cause and effect	Emphasizes the relationship between inputs and outputs, providing explanations or reasons for phenomena.
Compare and contrast	Holds two or more ideas alongside one another, showing how they are similar or different.
Problem-response	Identifies a complication and offers a path toward a resolution.

In the case of the internship initiative, there are a few ways you could go. For the sake of this example, let's play out what a *problem-response* narrative structure might look like. Imagine for instance the difference between these two examples.

Example 1, which "tells it by the numbers" and employs a low-narrativity approach:

> "Good morning and welcome to this quarterly review of outreach and recruitment data for our internship program. As you see on the slide, we were able to reach over 3000 college students across the region via our marketing campaign. From that we received 243 declarations of interest and 92 applications for the 25 internship opportunities available this year. The final demographic composition of the cohort was 70% white, 14% Hispanic or Latino, 12% Black or African American, and 4% Native Hawaiian or Other Pacific Islander. These data are at odds with community demographics, which I will now break down as follows..."

Example 2, which uses a high-narrativity approach to frame the pertinent data and present the complication at the heart of the challenge:

> "I want to talk to you about a young man called Michael. Here's a picture of Michael at his college graduation. He was the first in his family to go to college, taking on significant debt in the process, and having to work multiple jobs along the way to help cover expenses. Despite graduating at the top of his class, he's finding it almost impossible to find a job because he lacks the necessary work experience, and now his loan payments have begun. I want to suggest to you that our internship is made for young people like Michael and that we could be doing so much more to support him and other talented college graduates of color. We are located within a richly diverse community but we are failing to tap into that richness in the way we have constructed our intern recruitment pipeline – after all, the number of university graduates of color who join our internship cohort has averaged out at around 30% over the last three years, when the actual number in this community is closer to 70%. Since we know that our internship programs play a pivotal role in shaping the future workforce of the company (around 80% of our interns end up joining us in full-time roles), we stand to become less and less representative of the communities we serve and miss out on a hugely talented new generation – *unless* we do something to change this pattern. Thankfully, there are tangible strategic steps we can take to acknowledge, address, and reverse..."

Step 2: Decide on the 'Goldilocks Zone' Moments in Your Story

We know from research into causal coherence that if you want to present information in a way that demands memorable attention, you need to establish productive tension between cause and effect. Which is where the Goldilocks principle comes in.

Remember, the key here is to find the sweet spot between redundantly obvious and the inaccessibly obscure, while inviting the audience to "do some work" in connecting to the idea at the center. In our internship initiative example, one such Goldilocks moment might look like this:

- **Too obscure:** "In conclusion, I want to leave you with this: The actions we take today will have an effect on the future of this organization."
- **To obvious/explicit:** "In conclusion, I want to leave you with this: If we can decide on the right recruitment practices and get the right people in the door then that will mean we will become more institutionally diverse

over time, which in turn will mean that we better reflect the diversity of the community in which we live, which will mean we have met one of our key targets around attracting diverse new talent into the organization."

- **Just right:** "In conclusion, I want to leave you with this: The recruitment choices we make today will shape the diversity of the company and the community we will become."

Conclusion

Beyond what the research tells us about the utilitarian importance of storytelling, it is hard to ignore that there is something innately and instinctively human about this way of communicating. In the words of Marshall Ganz, whose own work on public narrative served as an inspiration to Barack Obama when he first ran for president:

> "Stories are told. They are not a disembodied string of words, images, and phrases. They are not messages, sound bites, or brands, although these rhetorical fragments may reference a story. Storytelling is fundamentally relational. ... Narrative allows us to communicate the emotional content of our values. Narrative is not talking 'about' values; rather, narrative embodies and communicates those values. It is through the shared experience of our values that we can engage with others; motivate one another to act; and find the courage to take risks, explore possibility, and face the challenges we must face."

If you can learn to wield the power of narratives in ways conducive to how the mind makes meaning and remembers, this most human of activities can become a truly powerful tool.

Takeaways

- Researchers have shown how texts can possess higher or lower "narrativity" in the way they are constructed. The higher the narrativity, the more memorable the information found within.
- An important aspect of narrativity is causal coherence, which explains the extent to which pieces of information can be connected through inference (i.e. noticing how one part relates to another).
- Evidence suggests that there is a sweet spot of causal coherence in which the connection between cause and effect is neither too obscure nor too obvious. This sweet spot renders the moment more memorable since the reader/listener must pay more attention and engage in deeper processing to infer the relationship between cause and effect.

- Using typical narrative structures (including specifically recognizable stories from culture) helps people to engage with, understand, and make memorable those texts.

References and further reading

Arya, D. J., & Maul, A. (2012). The role of the scientific discovery narrative in middle school science education: An experimental study. *Journal of Educational Psychology, 104*(4), 1022–1032.

Chen, Z., Mo, L., & Honomichl, R. (2004). Having the memory of an elephant: Long-term retrieval and the use of analogues in problem solving. *Journal of Experimental Psychology: General, 133*(3), 415–433.

Duffy, S. A., Shinjo, M., & Myers, J. L. (1990). The effect of encoding task on memory for sentence pairs varying in causal relatedness. *Journal of Memory and Language, 29*(1), 27–42.

Ganz, M. (2011). Public narrative, collective action, and power. In S. Odugbemi & T. Lee (eds.) *Accountability Through Public Opinion: From Inertia to Public Action*. Washington, DC: The World Bank, pp. 273–289.

Hohwy, J. (2013). *The Predictive Mind*. Oxford: Oxford University Press.

Keenan, J. M., Baillet, S. D., & Brown, P. (1984). The effect of causal cohesion on comprehension and memory. *Journal of Verbal Learning and Verbal Behavior, 23*(2), 115–126.

Meyer, B. J. F. (1975). *The Organization of Prose and its Effects on Memory*. Amsterdam: North-Holland.

Meyer, B. J. F., & Freedle, R. O. (1984) Effects of discourse type on recall. *American Educational Research Journal, 21*(1), 121–143.

Pyle, N., et al. (2017). Effects of expository text structure interventions on comprehension: A meta-analysis. *Reading Research Quarterly, 52*(4), 469–501.

8. MANAGING GROWTH: HOW EFFECTIVE PRACTICE BUILDS EXPERTISE

A local community theater is putting together a new production. They've held auditions to cast each role, the crew has been decided, and there are five weeks until opening night. How will they prepare?

Most of us know the answer to this question: Rehearsal. If we told you instead that their first time running lines or blocking scenes was opening night, you'd probably cringe knowing performing without practice is a recipe for disaster. The fact that clichés like "practice makes perfect" exist indicates there's wide consensus that practice is important. Writer Malcolm Gladwell popularized this further with the "10,000-hour rule" in his book *Outliers* – the idea that it takes 10,000 hours of practice to gain expertise.

But not all practice is created equal. Researchers have repeatedly shown it's possible to practice for hundreds of hours without any real improvement. How do we avoid this fate?

In reality, the *way* we practice matters. In order to improve performance, researchers have found we need to engage in specific types of practice and avoid others. That's why that 10,000-hour rule can't be taken at face value. One of the leading researchers on expertise, K. Anders Ericsson, and his colleagues defined three types of practice. Their work suggests two are key for building expertise and one, while common, isn't actually likely to help.

Types of Practice

Naive Practice

Naive practice, while prevalent, is not associated with improvement. It involves simply engaging in activities related to what you want to improve in without specific goals, sequenced structured practice activities, or feedback. For example, at the community theater, everyone running lines from the beginning of the play over and over is not effective practice. It's just repetition. At home, playing softball with friends or cooking dinner on a Tuesday night, while possibly enjoyable, isn't likely to bring you closer to being a world-class athlete or chef.

We often inadvertently buy into the myth of naive practice at work. It's easy to feel that by doing our jobs, especially given the long hours many of us put in, we are building skill. Unfortunately, research suggests this is not the case.

In a 2008 study, researchers Brorson and Hróbjartsson wanted to test whether experience could be equated with expertise. They showed groups of doctors test results and asked them whether the results indicated a bone was fractured. They expected to see that doctors with an orthopedic specialization (which requires additional years of training focused on bones, joints, ligaments, nerves, and tendons) would be likely to see the same data and agree on whether or not the bone was fractured. The assumption was that if expertise and experience were equivalent, the additional years of training would set up doctors with an orthopedic specialization to read the specialized data and accurately diagnose whether or not there was a fracture.

Instead, they found that doctors with an orthopedic specialization were no more likely to reach agreement on whether test results indicated a fracture than doctors without an orthopedic specialization. In other words, more time diagnosing fractured bones did not equate to more expertise. Interestingly, the researchers found that structured training aligned with the principles of purposeful practice (more on this later) improved the agreement of both the specialist *and* non-specialist groups of doctors.

What does this mean for the rest of us? The quality of our training matters. While preparing for an upcoming high-stakes meeting or identifying and fixing an issue with a product might be part of your role, without structured practice and feedback, it's unlikely to help you improve. Put another way, putting in more hours on the job isn't likely to make you any better at it, unless those hours are spent in a very specific way.

Deliberate Practice

According to Ericsson and his colleagues, deliberate practice is the most effective type of practice for building expertise. In order for practice to qualify as "deliberate practice," it must be guided by an expert coach. The coach:

- Sets the sequence for practice so that as the trainee masters more foundational elements, training tasks become increasingly complex

- Names goals for each training exercise
- Provides explicit instructions about the best way to do a given training exercise
- Carefully monitors practice, providing individualized feedback
- Offers remediation exercises to help a trainee improve in areas where they are struggling
- Ensures the trainee has multiple opportunities to engage with each training exercise
- Determines when the person is ready to move on to a more complex training task.

In order to do all this, the coach needs tremendous expertise in the domain.

You might have guessed this while reading this list but deliberate practice is not necessarily known for being fun. It takes intense concentration and an openness to frequent, corrective feedback. It also requires a willingness to engage in highly directed training. That is not to say it can't be satisfying. The goal of this type of practice is to efficiently build expertise, and across a variety of fields researchers have found it's the most effective way to do so.

What does this actually look like? Let's return to our group at the community theater. The director isn't going to gather everyone together on day one of rehearsal and say, "From the top," and then have the group practice the full production over and over. Instead, they're likely to focus on one scene, or even a single line of dialogue at a time. Only once they've mastered that will the director have the group progress to more complex scenes or begin to put sequences of scenes together. An effective director will provide individualized instructions on what various cast and crew members should attend to in a given rehearsal. They will also provide "notes," or feedback between attempts, and identify what participants should focus on when they practice at home between rehearsals.

Of course, not everyone has access to an expert coach. The reality is that many of us may not have access to anyone with expertise in the area where we are trying to build skill. Luckily, Ericsson and colleagues noted another type of practice that, while not as effective as deliberate practice with an expert coach, is still associated with performance gains.

Purposeful Practice

Purposeful practice is another effective way to build skill. To meet the requirements for "purposeful practice" a practice session needs to meet the following criteria:

- The task must be well defined with a clear goal
- The learner needs to understand both the task and the goal
- The learner needs the opportunity to perform the exercise several times, which creates opportunities for improvement and to build automaticity
- The learner needs a way to get immediate feedback on each attempt so they can make appropriate adjustments to improve.

What separates purposeful from deliberate practice is that purposeful practice is directed by the learner. The learner engages with activities designed to build specific skills. However, they don't have a coach to provide real-time feedback and direction. Instead, they might self-analyze their performance in relation to expert performance or specific criteria. For example, chess players can build skill by studying the opening moves of historic chess games, selecting what they think is the next best move, and comparing their decision to that of the actual chess masters who played or a computer-identified best move.

Returning to our example of community theater, if one of the actors wanted to engage in purposeful practice, we might imagine them going home between rehearsals and watching a video of a Broadway performance of the play. They might pause the video to map how the professional performer moves across the stage to convey emotion in a given scene. If they then attempt this multiple times themselves, each time trying to get closer to the movements they diagrammed, this is an example of purposeful practice. Likewise, if they rehearse a dialogue exchange by carefully comparing their language and delivery to the actor playing their character on video, noting areas for improvement and then trying their dialogue again, this would be another example of purposeful practice.

While purposeful practice like this can be effective, it hinges on the learner being able to do several things. They need to be able to accurately assess their own performance, identify the most important areas for improvement, and know what to do to get better. Unfortunately these are all things researchers have shown novices notoriously struggle with, which is why deliberate practice is more effective.

Now that you know what Ericsson's three types of practice are, let's dig into some of the components of deliberate and purposeful practice and what makes them effective.

What Makes Some Practice More Effective than Others?

Sequencing Practice

You'll hear more about sequencing in a later chapter, but for deliberate and purposeful practice to each be effective, they have to be broken into bite-sized exercises that are sequenced from simple to complex. This is because our working memory has limited capacity. There's so much to focus on when you are trying something new that it's common to experience cognitive overload or pay attention to the wrong thing. This is why sequencing practice is especially important for novices.

Sequencing from simple to complex lets you start by building automaticity with the more basic elements of what you are working on. Once you've practiced enough, those are stored as "chunks" in long-term memory that can be called up when you need them. As a result, they no longer take up as much space in working memory, and this opens up room for you to focus on more complex skills during your practice sessions. It's for this reason that a director may have actors work single lines of dialogue before they move to full scenes and then sequences of scenes. However, careful sequencing isn't the only reason purposeful and deliberate practice are each effective.

Accurate Assessment of Performance

Low performers notoriously overestimate their competence. This tendency toward being "unskilled and unaware" has been dubbed the Dunning–Kruger effect after the two researchers who published some of the seminal work on this unfortunate trend. Researchers have found the Dunning–Kruger effect to be true across a variety of domains, including humor, grammar, and interview skills. They've also found it to hold across different groups of participants, ranging from undergraduate students to physicians (this may give you pause next time your doctor shares a prognosis with confidence).

Dunning and Kruger posited this has to do, in part, with novices' lack of expertise. Novices simply don't have the schemas that would allow them to discriminate poor from excellent performance. In one study of logical reasoning using something called a Wason selection task, Dunning and Kruger found that the lowest-performing participants thought they scored in the 55th percentile on the task when, in fact, they scored in the 12th. A week later the researchers had participants attend a training session focused on solving Wason tasks. Afterward, they asked participants to re-rate their prior performance. After becoming more skilled, participant ratings of their original performance were harsher, and importantly, more accurate. This suggests the more expertise we gain, the more realistically we can gauge our own performance. This is also why we might not want to trust our perceptions of how we did on a given task, and why feedback from an expert coach can be so powerful.

Corrective and Directive Feedback

An expert coach can help learners know what to cut and what to keep in order to improve. Research on effective feedback has found corrective and directive feedback is particularly useful for novices. Corrective feedback helps novices see where they can improve. Directive feedback tells them what to do instead. For example, a director might say to their lighting crew, "On this next round, move the spotlight about a foot this way so that the audience's gaze will be drawn stage left."

Sometimes we can shy away from giving this type of feedback because we worry we will be perceived as unkind or overbearing. However, when we do this we are actually shortchanging the people we claim to want to support by withholding the type of feedback that will help them most. You'll align with best practices if your feedback is specific, focused on the task not the person, and delivered in a warm tone.

Verification Feedback

It's also important for a coach to explicitly name for the learner what they are doing well (e.g. "Yes! On this next take, dim the light at the same pace as his exit, just like last time"). Labeling what's in line with the target performance will help ensure that the learner continues to do those things. Because of their limited schemas, novices may not even realize they've done something effective. Likewise, they may focus so much on trying to correct errors that they lose what's working well.

Notice that while we've discussed verifying what's working well and the role of corrective feedback, we haven't talked about having learners reflect on their practice. Because their self-assessments are often inaccurate, when novices only engage in open-ended reflection, and don't have the opportunity to receive directive, corrective, and verifying feedback from an expert coach, it's not associated with improvement in performance.

We share this because opening up space for reflection, rather than giving direct feedback, is incredibly common. This may be because it feels "nicer" (at least in the short term) to both parties. If we are honest, it also takes less work to ask a generic open-ended question than craft effective feedback. This isn't to say there is no space for questions like "How do you think that went?" or "How did it feel?" These give space for processing so the learner feels heard and can give you a sense of the accuracy of their self-perception. However, if *all* you do is support reflection, the research is clear that you shouldn't expect to see people you support make rapid progress.

Opportunities to Refine Mental Models

There's one final reason feedback from an expert coach is key. Feedback helps a learner refine their mental model of the desired outcome. Each time the coach points out a similarity or difference between the learner's current performance and the target, the learner's understanding of the target (their mental model) improves.

This feedback is most effective when it's given as elaborative feedback, drawing the learner's attention to *why* something is effective or ineffective in helping achieve their goal. For example, imagine that in the previous example the director said, "Dim the light at the same pace as his exit, just like last time. It helps us efficiently end the scene." In addition to ensuring the lighting crew does the same thing on the next take, the addition of "it helps us efficiently end the scene" helps the crew build schemas for the way lighting impacts the timeline of a performance. They're building expertise that will assist them in this *and* future productions.

Refined mental models come with additional benefits. Once a learner has an accurate mental model for their desired outcome, their ability to self-assess improves. This means they are able to engage in more effective independent, purposeful practice.

So now you have a sense for why purposeful and deliberate practice are effective ways to build skill. Before we jump into our mental model for this chapter, we want to address a couple of common misconceptions related to practice.

When Practice Goes Wrong

In the workplace, practice can go wrong in a variety of ways. We've already discussed naive practice – simply doing your job isn't going to necessarily make you better at it. Unfortunately, there are several other ways people ineffectively try to build skill in the workplace. We want to quickly call out two because they are so pervasive.

Let's Talk About It

We used the example of putting on a play in this chapter because, in the context of theater, people tend to equate practice with rehearsal. However, in most workplaces the majority of skill-building opportunities do not include rehearsal. Instead, they fall into the trap of talking about improvement, rather than *practicing* to improve.

For example, imagine a workplace that wants managers to improve their feedback conversations. Following principles of deliberate practice, they might have managers role-play a feedback conversation. They'd follow the role-plays with feedback on what worked well and what to improve before asking managers to try the conversation again.

Instead, many organizations do something like this: "We'd like all managers to read this article on effective feedback conversations. Next week, we've put time on the calendar to discuss what we've learned and how we might apply some of these ideas in our work."

Here's why this doesn't work. If you are a manager in this organization, the procedure you practice and encode in long-term memory (reading an article, navigating workplace book club dynamics, and wowing your colleagues with your insights) is **not** the procedure you need in real life (leading an effective feedback conversation). There are a lot of managers who can talk about feedback; whether they can deliver it effectively is an entirely different question. The takeaway? Talking about something is **not** the same as actually practicing it. Practice like you'll play. If you want to build skill, make sure you get to *actually practice* the thing you need to be able to do.

Stopping at Level 1

While some workplaces are providing opportunities for more aligned, authentic practice, many times these practice opportunities fall short of the complexity of real life. Let's say an organization provides managers an opportunity to role-play leading a performance conversation following guidelines outlined in a template. If managers only get to practice conversations that align exactly with the template, they are likely to struggle in real life when someone who directly reports to you disagrees with their evaluation or becomes upset they didn't get a promotion they expected. While you can't practice for every scenario, it is important to approximate responding to challenges you can reasonably expect to encounter. Without opportunities to do this, you'll only store the most basic part of the procedures you need in long-term memory, which may leave you unprepared for the rigor of the real thing. Let's see how you can apply this through our next mental model.

Effective Practice in Practice

Big Idea: Build expertise through effective practice.

Mental Model: Tending the Garden.

Whether you are coaching little league soccer or managing a team of 12, think of yourself as a gardener who has been charged with supporting each individual's growth.

Wanting to grow expertise on your team? Here's what that might look like.

Imagine someone who reports to you needs to improve their presentations in internal meetings. They rarely get through key information because they spend too much time building context and are often sidetracked by questions. In addition, you've received feedback from other teams that when this person presents at a meeting, attendees either a) tune out or b) feel frustrated because the presentations take so long that there isn't time for dialogue or decision making.

We'll walk you through a cycle you can use to design effective practice opportunities to help others build skill.

Step 1: Build a Trellis to Direct the Growth

Just like a trellis supports a plant and shows it the direction you want it to grow, you've got to support and direct your colleague's practice. Set up a clear practice task and state its goal. Then spell out what the person should do during the practice session and why. This includes outlining what the learner should be focused on. You should also plan to model how to do it or give them a process they can use when they try it on their own. For example:

> "We've been talking about how a high-priority area for you is improving your presentations for the leadership team. We are going to start by distinguishing essential information from tertiary details. Too much information and people will miss or tune out your great points. I'll walk you through one way I decide what to share and what to leave out when I

present to this audience. I'll use the notes from last week's project meeting and explain my different choices about what I would cut and what I would keep. Your task for this week will be to use this process, pretending you need to update the leadership team after the upcoming project team meeting. I want you to come to our next 1:1 with your notes on what's essential to share and what's better left behind."

Note that this practice opportunity is outside of what might come up in the day-to-day job. You aren't simply waiting for the next time they have to present and calling it a learning opportunity. You want to give them practice opportunities now so they have the skills to be successful next time they have to create a presentation.

You also aren't asking them to practice everything all at once. You've chunked the practice to focus on one thing at a time. This week they might focus on identifying what they do and don't need to communicate, next week on pacing their presentations, and so on.

With the practice activity complete, you are ready to move to step 2.

Step 2: Water What Works

There's a phrase: "What you water grows." Protect what's working well. Just as watering a plant protects it from drought, strengthens it, and gives it the resources it needs to grow, you want to provide your learner with feedback that protects the things that are working well. Verifying the elements of their performance that are in line with the target builds motivation. It also ensures they don't forget these elements because they are focusing so intently on what they need to improve. You want to name it so it isn't lost.

In the example above, after your colleague shares their list of what they think is (and isn't) essential to communicate in a leadership update, providing feedback that protects what's working well might sound like this: "Your second point is exactly in line with what we talked about. Leadership needs to know that if we make the proposed budget cuts it will delay project completion."

Then, remember to include *why* what they are doing is effective. For example, "The side-by-side timelines you created for each budget scenario will help the leadership team easily weigh the trade-offs of different budget cuts." This elaborative feedback builds their mental model for the desired outcome. This, in turn, will support their practice with you and their ability to effectively practice on their own.

Of course, it's likely that they aren't going to master everything on their first attempt. When supporting novices with building new skills, you also need to label what's not working and provide them with direction for how to improve. This takes us to the next stage of the cycle: Prune.

Step 3: Prune What's Not Working

Gardening can feel counterintuitive because one of the ways you support healthy growth is by pruning. When we prune, we remove parts of the plant that are growing in the wrong direction or are unhealthy. Shearing these off opens up resources that the plant can put into new, healthy growth. This is remarkably similar to the role corrective feedback plays when we are supporting novice learners.

Remember, novices don't yet have the schemas to be able to identify the highest leverage things to cut or change, nor are they going to know the most effective way to fix them. Help them course correct when they need to. The less expertise the person you are working with has, the more you should expect to do this.

What does this sound like? After providing feedback designed to protect what's working, you might say something like "Your first point, where you outline all your proposals for mitigating each risk to project completion, is still too much information. I don't want people to tune you out. Let's start by asking ourselves 'What information is this audience looking for and what will they do with it?' We'll use that as our guide and go through your list and see what, if anything, is essential to communicate."

After you've provided this feedback, you are ready to start the cycle again. The first step will be to direct their next practice activity. You'll have to decide – do they need more practice with this same skill or are they ready for the next step in the progression? Given that they are still struggling to match information to the audience, they likely need another attempt with this practice activity. This is normal. Once they've mastered this skill, you can move to other skills that will help them improve their presentations.

A quick final thought. Notice that in this example the practice activity was using information from an actual project meeting to determine what is essential to communicate. We didn't suggest that you should send the person you manage to a webinar about engaging presentations and then ask them how it was in your next 1:1. It's not that webinars or other professional development are inherently bad. However, *receiving information is different from practicing an actual job-specific task*. If we want to help others build expertise, we have to be sure their learning includes actual practice.

Conclusion

Effective practice is hard. It requires a lot of work from the trainee and the expert coach who is facilitating it. Here are a few points to remember.

Takeaways

- Remember, time ≠ improvement, unless that time is spent in very particular ways. Naive practice, simply doing activities in the domain you want to improve, isn't associated with performance gains. If you want to build expertise, engage in purposeful or deliberate practice that is carefully sequenced, has clear goals, provides multiple attempts for mastery, and includes opportunities for feedback.
- Novices will need more help. People who are in the early stages of building expertise rarely have an accurate perception of their own performance. The tendency of low-performers of being "unskilled and unaware" has been dubbed the Dunning–Kruger effect and has been found to be true across a variety of domains, including humor, grammar, and interview skills.
- There are a few types of feedback that are especially useful as you build a new skill. Corrective feedback helps novices see where they can improve. Directive feedback tells them what to stop and what to do instead. Verification feedback names for the learner what they are doing well and should continue. Elaborative feedback draws the learner's attention to why something is effective or ineffective in helping achieve their goal.

References and further reading

Brorson, S., & Hróbjartsson, A. (2008). Training improves agreement among doctors using the Neer system for proximal humeral fractures in a systematic review. *Journal of Clinical Epidemiology, 61*(1), 7–16.

Cohen, J., Wong, V., Krishnamachari, A., & Berlin, R. (2020). Teacher coaching in a simulated environment. *Educational Evaluation and Policy Analysis, 42*(2), 208–231.

Dania, A., Kaltsonoudi, K., Ktistakis, I., Trampa, K., Boti, N., & Pesce, C. (2023). Chess training for improving executive functions and invasion game tactical behavior of college student athletes: A preliminary investigation. *Physical Education and Sport Pedagogy, 28*(4), 380–396.

Debatin, T., Hopp, M. D., Vialle, W., & Ziegler, A. (2023). The meta-analyses of deliberate practice underestimate the effect size because they neglect the core characteristic of individualization—An analysis and empirical evidence. *Current Psychology, 42*(13), 10815–10825.

Dunning, D. (2011). The Dunning–Kruger effect: On being ignorant of one's own ignorance. In J. M. Olson, & M. P. Zanna. *Advances in Experimental Social Psychology*, Vol. 44. San Diego, CA: Academic Press, pp. 247–296.

Ericsson, K. A. (2016). Summing up hours of any type of practice versus identifying optimal practice activities: Commentary on Macnamara, Moreau, & Hambrick (2016). *Perspectives on Psychological Science, 11*(3), 351–354.

Ericsson, K. A. (2021). Given that the detailed original criteria for deliberate practice have not changed, could the understanding of this complex concept have improved over time? A response to Macnamara and Hambrick (2020). *Psychological Research, 85*(3), 1114–1120.

Ericsson, K. A., & Harwell, K. W. (2019). Deliberate practice and proposed limits on the effects of practice on the acquisition of expert performance: Why the original definition matters and recommendations for future research. *Frontiers in Psychology, 10*, 2396.

Ericsson, K. A., Krampe, R. T., & Tesch-Römer, C. (1993). The role of deliberate practice in the acquisition of expert performance. *Psychological Review, 100*(3), 363.

Harwell, K., & Southwick, D. (2021). Beyond 10,000 hours: Addressing misconceptions of the expert performance approach. *Journal of Expertise, 4*(2), 220–233.

Hodges, B., Regehr, G., & Martin, D. (2001). Difficulties in recognizing one's own incompetence: Novice physicians who are unskilled and unaware of it. *Academic Medicine, 76*(10), S87–S89.

Krampe, R. T., & Ericsson, K. A. (1996). Maintaining excellence: Deliberate practice and elite performance in young and older pianists. *Journal of Experimental Psychology: General, 125*(4), 331–359.

Kruger, J., & Dunning, D. (1999). Unskilled and unaware of it: How difficulties in recognizing one's own incompetence lead to inflated self-assessments. *Journal of Personality and Social Psychology, 77*(6), 1121–1134.

Moxley, J. H., Ericsson, K. A., & Tuffiash, M. (2019). Gender differences in SCRABBLE performance and associated engagement in purposeful practice activities. *Psychological Research, 83*, 1147–1167.

National Research Council. (2000). *How People Learn: Brain, Mind, Experience, and School: Expanded Edition.* Washington, DC: The National Academies Press.

Shute, V. J. (2008). Focus on formative feedback. *Review of Educational Research, 78*(1), 153–189.

PART 4

THE WEIGHT OF THOUGHT: WORKING MEMORY AND COGNITIVE LOAD

This section digs deeper into cognitive load theory. We look at how you can use it to "game" the learning process and to avoid creating situations where thinking breaks down.

9. AVOID OVERLOAD: MANAGING THE LIMITATIONS OF WORKING MEMORY

It's happened to all of us. You are about to walk out the door for work and you realize you are going to have to hit every light perfectly if you don't want to be late. You start calculating the fastest route at this time of morning. Meanwhile, you grab your work bag and rummage to make sure you have your wallet. Remembering your lunch, you double back to the kitchen and grab it with your free hand. You finally head back to the door, nestling a travel mug of coffee and your phone under the other arm. As you open the door, the dog tries to make a run for it, so you try to block it with one leg. "Don't forget the boxes you said you were going to drop at the post office on the way home," your partner calls, while somehow managing to wedge two boxes into your already full arms. You finally make it outside and just as you are trying to lock the door behind you, the inevitable happens.

First, your coffee hits the stoop. Within milliseconds, the rest is tumbling down.

While maybe your morning exits are less dramatic than ours, this process – where more balls keep getting added for you to juggle until they all come crashing down – is remarkably similar to what happens when thinking breaks down in working memory. In this chapter we will dig into what working memory is, its role in cognition, and how to avoid cognitive overload.

As you may remember from chapter 1, working memory plays a critical role in cognition. In working memory, we combine information from our environment with information from long-term memory. The result is stored in long-term memory. There's a lot of cognitive science vocabulary in that last sentence so here's an example of what that might look like.

Imagine you are driving. The environment is filled with audio, visual, and other sensory stimuli. So when, for example, you suddenly notice a loud, repeating, high-pitched sound in your environment, that sound is moved into working memory. Processing quickly, you might pull from long-term memory that the sound is a siren. "Oh," you might think, "I need to look for a good spot to pull over."

Working memory is the site where meaning-making occurs. It's where the new information from your environment (loud, high-pitched sound) was processed using information stored in long-term memory ("I bet that's a siren"). You were able to use this to decide what to do next ("I need to pull over!").

This is all assuming you don't experience cognitive overload. Unfortunately, working memory capacity is limited. When you take in too much at once, information competes for space and some is lost. This is termed "interference."

So let's imagine you are back driving that car, only this time your child is talking to you from the backseat. If you are deeply engaged in what they are saying, it may take you a moment to notice the sirens because your working memory is filled with anecdotes of what happened at school. On the other hand, even if your child continues chattering away after you've recognized the sirens, once you start trying to figure out how to merge across multiple lines of traffic to pull over, it's unlikely you'll hear a word they're saying. There's too much information for your mind to hold it all at once.

Researchers also believe information can decay from working memory, gone because it wasn't processed quickly enough. You've learned about techniques for effortful processing in earlier chapters. Another common way we process information to avoid decay is by rehearsing it. For example, imagine as you're driving, your partner calls to ask you to pick up a few items for dinner on the way home. Normally, you might repeat the shopping list in your head until you can write it down. However, if the sirens start up and you have to focus on merging and pulling over before you can rehearse the list in your head, it's likely you'll arrive at the store with no idea of what you were supposed to buy. The information decayed from working memory because it was never processed.

All of this is because attention and working memory are limited resources. While it varies by person and depends on the task, studies have shown that most of us can hold a maximum of only seven chunks (give or take two) of information in working memory. Researchers have also found that if information isn't processed within approximately 30 seconds, it's lost.

You can experience this for yourself. Without writing anything down, try to recite the days of the week alphabetically. It was probably tough, but ultimately doable. Again, don't write anything down, but this time try to alphabetize the months of the year. This was probably harder.

Why? In the first task, you had to hold the seven pieces of information (days of the week) in working memory. Even if you were able to call these up as one chunk of information from long-term memory, you added additional items to working memory when you started alphabetizing. For example, knowing Thursday is alphabetized before Tuesday requires holding the first two letters of each word in working memory. You also had to simultaneously hold steps for putting things in alphabetical order in working memory and use working memory space for shuffling the order of the days of the week. For the months of the year, the demands are the same, but you are starting with 12 pieces of information rather than seven. That's a recipe for cognitive overload.

The world is already full of difficult tasks (we're sure you regularly have to do more complex work than alphabetizing) and constant distractions competing for our attention. We do ourselves no favors by unwittingly adding attention-sucking behaviors to the mix.

Researchers have debunked the myth of multitasking. While it may feel like you can do two things at once, studies have shown that what many of us call "multitasking" is actually rapid attention switching between tasks. This comes with a cost. Attention and working memory are limited resources. The more you attend to one thing, the less you attend to another. This is why it's worth reconsidering leaving your chat open during focused work time or emailing during a meeting. Not only will your attention be yanked back and forth between your work and messages, but the information from both will start piling up in working memory. Once there's too much, all that information will compete for space and some will be lost. You're leaving to chance whether the most important information makes it into long-term memory or you miss it entirely. This is also why you should feel justified giving your child a side eye if they tell you they do their homework best with the TV on in the background.

There's one more problem with cognitive overload. It doesn't feel very good. Think back to how you felt trying to alphabetize the months of the year without visual aids. It likely felt taxing, even frustrating. In fact, researchers have found experiencing cognitive overload repeatedly can undermine motivation. Therefore, it's something we want to ensure we're not regularly experiencing or causing in other people. Next, we'll review a few ways we can avoid cognitive overload. We'll start by breaking down cognitive load, which researchers have categorized into three types: Extraneous, intrinsic, and germane.

Extraneous Load

Extraneous load refers to the unnecessary load caused by things that are not essential to a task. Extraneous load often stems from the way we present information. For example, if you watch a how-to video with animated illustrations that are growing, shrinking, flashing, and bouncing, you'll use working memory space trying to track the animation rather than processing the information in the video. Doesn't that mean it's engaging? The animation is certainly capturing your attention, but it's adding to the cognitive load of the task in ways that have nothing to do with its goal.

Distractions in the environment can also add unnecessary cognitive load. If you are typing away and hear your name mentioned in a nearby conversation, suddenly your working memory will be filled with questions like "Why would they be talking about me?" You can also tax working memory by focusing on what isn't there. For example, if you are sitting in a meeting trying to guess "What is this meeting about?" you have less space for processing what people are saying.

Intrinsic Load

Intrinsic load refers to the demands of the task itself. This includes the task's "element interactivity" or the number of things someone needs to know and be able to do to complete the task (what cognitive scientists call the task elements) and how interrelated they are. Calling back to one of our earlier examples, listing the months of the year has low element interactivity. This is because your ability to recall one month doesn't hinge on whether or not you can recall another (e.g. you might remember there's a month called February, even if you can't remember there's one called November). Alphabetizing the months of the year has higher element interactivity because knowing where November sits in the sequence requires you to be able to list, spell, and sequence this and the other months.

Germane Load

Germane load refers to the cognitive load required for knowledge acquisition from the task. It's the amount of working memory capacity required to move information from working memory to long-term memory. You've learned about this in previous chapters when we talked about how deeply processing information (for example, by asking yourself "how" or "why" questions) makes it more likely you'll be able to remember it later.

So, how does knowing there are different types of cognitive load help? There are multiple ways to get around the limits of working memory, some of which will be covered in later chapters. For this chapter, we'll focus on one thing. If you understand the types of cognitive load, you can be savvy about the way you use working memory's valuable real estate and avoid cognitive overload. Here's what researchers recommend.

Minimize Extraneous Load

If you want learners to remember what you say, keep distractions to a minimum. Forget antitrust laws here. You want the information they need to learn to have a total monopoly on working memory space. Squash the competition by cutting out anything unrelated.

Instructional design researchers call these seductive details, and we'll discuss them more in chapter 15. For now, we'll say that seductive details, while potentially interesting, are unnecessary to achieving your instructional aim. In our work, we've both observed college professors who fall prey to using seductive details when, in a well-intentioned effort to connect to students, they litter their slides with memes and GIFs. While sometimes these get students to laugh, they rarely help them understand the material better. With few exceptions, decades of research have found that people learn more from instructional experiences that do not include these details as opposed to those that do.

Nike executives popularized the phrase "edit to amplify." That maxim applies here. By removing distracting elements of a learner's task, you open up space in working memory for deep processing of what's most important.

Shrink the Scope

Sometimes the intrinsic demands of a task are just too big for a learner's working memory. This is especially true when they are trying something new. There's a phrase that's often used in schools: "No multistep directions." It's the idea that you can't read out a multistep process, like a nine-step dismissal procedure, and expect listeners to be able to execute it the first time. It's more than anyone's working memory can hold. Instead, you shrink the scope by giving one direction at a time, effectively reducing the task from nine elements to one. The intrinsic load of a series of single-step directions like "First, put your science folder in your backpack. Great work" and "Next, line up behind your table leader" is a lot more fair than droning your way through an unbroken paragraph of all the things they need to do to get from their desk to the bus. This isn't just true in elementary school. We hope you'll think twice before firing off a long, complicated to-do list to a person who reports to you as you hurry between meetings.

One more note before we move into this chapter's mental model. You may be wondering how all this talk of reducing cognitive load squares with what you heard in previous chapters about the importance of effortful thinking and deep processing. Researchers call the latter "desirable difficulties." It's cognitive load well spent because it's the type of processing that ensures information actually makes it from working memory to long-term memory. By keeping the intrinsic load manageable and eliminating extraneous load (or *un*desirable difficulties), you can make sure there's plenty of working memory space for desirable, effortful processing.

Avoiding Overload in Practice

What does it actually take to avoid cognitive overload?

Big Idea: Working memory is a limited resource. Right-size your tasks and remove distractions to make space for what's important.

Mental Model: The Museum Curator.

We are calling this mental model the museum curator because the processes to create an excellent museum exhibit echo the processes you can use to manage cognitive load.

Step 1: Assess the Scope of the Exhibit

Before creating an exhibit, a curator needs to understand the breadth of material they could cover and what they ultimately want participants to walk away with. For example, imagine at a science museum the curator wants to ensure visitors leave knowing what makes something a planet, a few key characteristics of each planet in the solar system, and what makes each planet unique. In addition to the basics, they might also want to include information about why stars and moons are not considered planets and a history on the classification of Pluto. If they aren't careful, they could end up with too much information in one exhibit.

When you're "assessing the scope," it can be helpful to ask yourself:

- What do I need learners to engage with?
- How big is the task? How complex is it?

The greater the scope, the more you'll need the steps below.

Step 2: Edit and Curate

A museum curator has to make hard decisions like this all the time. While they may have access to a series of rocket engines from recent expeditions to the international space station, a curator will make the decision to save those for a future exhibit that focuses on space travel. This way, the artifacts and multimedia they have related to each planet have space to shine.

When you "edit and curate," remind yourself:

- Working memory is a limited resource. Be ruthless with what you cut. Remember, every item you add is competing with what you want people to be thinking about. Unrelated? Let it go. Not the highest priority? Not worth it.
- Edit to amplify. By carefully curating what you put in front of people, you make it more likely they have the space to actually process what's most important and store it in long-term memory.

Step 3: Space It Out

Museums do this all the time. Rarely do you walk into an exhibit where everything is crammed together on a single shelf. This isn't because of a minimalist aesthetic. Rather, related items and information are grouped together and carefully spaced over multiple rooms so as not to overwhelm the viewer. Spacing items allows the viewer to focus and engage with each item individually, in addition to thinking about how the exhibit fits together as a whole. Each item is given room to shine.

When you're "spacing it out," think baby steps.

- Keep task size manageable by asking people to take on less at a time to avoid overload.
- Looking for an easy way to do this? Only introduce step 2 after your learner has completed step 1.

So what might this look like outside the walls of a museum?

Putting the Museum Curator into Practice

Imagine you've been tasked with leading sessions for different departments introducing your organization's new policies for event planning. You want participants to leave your session able to organize events in line with the new guidance, including criteria for selecting vendors, expected timelines and communication, budgeting, and submitting expense reports.

Assess the Scope

You know this session contains a lot of new information. Not only will you be introducing new processes that teams will need to use, but some will also require using new software. Because of the breadth of what you need to cover, you'll need to be extra attentive to the following steps.

Edit and Curate

Removing distractions that add unnecessary cognitive load can take a variety of forms:

- **Design:** Take a critical eye to your slides. Too much text? Distracting animation? Those are all burdening participants' working memories. Ruthlessly simplify.
- **Content:** Keep it tight. This isn't the time to preview fun bonus features in the software, nor is it the time for a long anecdote on the different budgeting programs the operations team considered and how they came to agree on this one. Focus on what is most important for participants to know so you don't add clutter to their working memory space.
- **Environment:** Ask attendees to close laptops so they won't be distracted by chats or email. Let them know that if they need to use them during the session to practice on the new platforms, you'll cue them. Remember, every time they get pinged, that's a tax on working memory.

Space It Out

If you present everything in the session to participants at once, you should prepare for glazed expressions and frustrated whispers. They are likely to experience cognitive overload.

Instead, shrink how much you ask participants to hold in their minds at a time. Give them time to process each piece of information so it's not lost to decay or interference when you introduce something new. Here's an example of what we don't and do mean:

- **No:** I'll demo the eight-step process for logging expenses on the new platform. You can look up a video later if you need a refresher.
- **Yes:** We are going to work through the new system for logging expenses. Let's start with step 1. I'll demo it, then we'll practice together. Great, onto step 2...

Pausing to build in time for participants to ask questions can also be helpful. It makes it more likely lingering questions aren't taking up extra space in working memory when you switch to a new topic. Conversely, you can also pause to ask participants questions before moving to a new idea, using what you learned about effortful thinking in chapter 5. This builds in processing time to make sure that information is moved to long-term memory before it's lost due to interference or decay.

Additional Considerations

We gave one example earlier, but the importance of understanding cognitive load theory is not limited to introducing new organizational processes. We are far from perfect and have definitely created environments where people experienced cognitive overload. Here are a few tips on how to avoid that:

- **Content Creation –**
    - When you are preparing slide decks newsletters, flyers, social media posts, videos, and emails spotlight the essentials, remove the rest. Keep content in digestible chunks.
- **Meetings –**
    - It's worth the time to share an agenda in advance so people don't use working memory space trying to guess where things are headed. It also helps ensure each agenda item is kept to a manageable size.
    - Be a minimalist with your invite list to avoid a lot of extraneous information being brought up.
    - Check your pre-reading. Is the whole document you sent relevant or would an excerpt or a couple of headlines be better? (Probably, the latter.)
- **Internal Decision Making –**
    - Shrink big, complex decisions to a series of smaller sub-decisions to manage the intrinsic load.
    - Constantly clarify the scope of the decision you are making (e.g. "We decided we are limiting this discussion to X and Y. I appreciate

you bringing up Z, and that's food for later thought, but for this conversation, it's extraneous").

- **Project Onboarding** – Is someone joining a new project? It's probably not helpful to send a link to the notes from the last four months of meetings. Not only is that not a good use of your new teammate's time (and will they even read it?), but it's also possible they will experience this as information overload. The notes likely contain a lot of extraneous information.
- **Emotional Management** – When people are thinking about how to manage their or others' emotions, this is taking up working memory space. This means they'll have less bandwidth for the content of the interaction. Make space for emotions and recognize when people may be at their limit. It may be helpful to meet another time.

Conclusion

Yes, working memory is limited, but this doesn't need to be *limiting*. If you trim extraneous details and segment learning into bite-sized pieces, you'll ensure learners have plenty of room to process what's important.

Takeaways

- Working memory is limited. When too much information is in working memory, we experience cognitive overload and thinking breaks down.
- Different things contribute to the cognitive load of a task:
    - Intrinsic load:
        - This is the complexity of the task itself.
        - Keep this manageable by segmenting big tasks into bite-sized pieces.
    - Extraneous load:
        - This is processing that is irrelevant to the task (e.g. watching an animation pulse on the screen).
        - Minimize distractions so learners have space to process what matters.
    - Germane load:
        - This is the processing that's required for knowledge acquisition.
        - This is necessary cognitive load. Make space for it using the tips discussed in this chapter.

References and further reading

Baddeley, A. (2001). Is working memory still working? *American Psychologist, 56*(11), 849–864.

Baddeley, A. D., & Hitch, G. J. (1974). Working memory. In G. Bower (ed.) *The Psychology of Learning and Motivation* (Vol. 8). New York: Academic Press.

Bjork, R. A., & Bjork, E. L. (2020). Desirable difficulties in theory and practice. *Journal of Applied Research in Memory and Cognition, 9*(4), 475–479.

Keppel, G., & Underwood, B. J. (1962). Proactive inhibition in short-term retention of single items. *Journal of Verbal Learning and Verbal Behavior, 1*(3), 153–161.

Mayer, R. E., & Moreno, R. (2003). Nine ways to reduce cognitive load in multimedia learning. *Educational Psychologist, 38*(1), 43–52.

McNew, B. S. (2017). *Why Nike CEO says "Less is more"*. The Motley Fool. Available at: www.fool.com/investing/2017/01/04/why-nike-ceo-says-less-is-more.aspx (Accessed: December 11, 2024).

Murdock Jr, B. B. (1967). Recent developments in short-term memory. *British Journal of Psychology, 58*(3–4), 421–433.

Paas, F., Renkl, A., & Sweller, J. (2003). Cognitive load theory and instructional design: Recent developments. *Educational Psychologist, 38*(1), 1–4.

Peterson, L., & Peterson, M. J. (1959). Short-term retention of individual verbal items. *Journal of Experimental Psychology, 58*(3), 193–198.

Reitman, J. S. (1971). Mechanisms of forgetting in short-term memory. *Cognitive Psychology, 2*(2), 185–195.

Serki, N., & Bolkan, S. (2024). The effect of clarity on learning: Impacting motivation through cognitive load. *Communication Education, 73*(1), 29–45.

Sweller, J. (1994). Cognitive load theory, learning difficulty, and instructional design. *Learning and Instruction, 4*(4), 295–312.

Sweller, J. (2010) Element interactivity and intrinsic, extraneous, and germane cognitive load. *Educational Psychology Review, 22*, 123–138.

Willingham, D. T., & Riener, C. (2019). *Cognition: The Thinking Animal.* Cambridge: Cambridge University Press.

10. CHANNEL SURFING: PROCESSING INFORMATION THROUGH VISUAL AND VERBAL CHANNELS

Rebekah isn't known for her understanding of liquid volume.

When preparing an already-large soup recipe, she and her husband, Matt, decided to double the amount because they were having people over for dinner and wanted enough leftovers to take to her grandparents over the weekend. They employed a divide-and-conquer approach: Rebekah handled the soup while Matt readied the house for guests.

Rebekah chopped aromatics and added them to the pot. She chopped vegetables and added them to the pot. She thought to herself, "A couple of cans of diced tomatoes would be nice," and so, in they went. Wanting to up the protein, she grabbed a few cans of beans and poured them in, too. Next came the broth. She poured jar after jar of stock into the increasingly full pot of soup. Realizing they had harvested more garden greens than they could eat that week, she chopped them up as another addition.

She was just beginning to stir the greens into the brimming pot, when Matt walked in and yelled, "Rebekah, no!" Soup started to cascade down the sides. Matt grabbed a second pot and poured half of the contents in.

Here's what Rebekah reflected on as she cleaned broth and vegetables off the stove top: Use two pots. The same amount of soup split between two vessels, means both can merrily simmer away without issue. No soup lost.

If you've made it this far in the book, you've probably guessed we didn't share this story because we have a passion for matching the right cookware to the right dish. Information entering our minds actually functions a lot like the soup in this story. We have multiple channels for processing information. When we flood one channel with information, we cause cognitive overload. But if we split the same information across multiple channels, we can process it without an issue. No soup lost.

The Dual-Channel Assumption

Cognitive scientists posit we have two channels through which we process information.[1] They are:

- **Visual:** Examples include images, diagrams, and written words.
- **Verbal:** Examples include dialogue and narration.

As you now know, working memory is limited (and if you don't know, see the previous chapter for a refresher). Exploiting your knowledge of the two ways we process information can help you get around the limits of working memory. On the other hand, if you don't understand the dual-channel assumption, you are likely to cause cognitive overload. Here's an example of what we mean by that.

Avoid Overload

Imagine you are trying to understand how your toilet works because you think it needs to be repaired and want to see if you can do it yourself. Online, you click on an article. There are a few paragraphs that explain what happens when a toilet is flushed, step by step. Each paragraph includes an animation.

Researchers have found this is a recipe for cognitive overload. You are flooding the visual channel with words (paragraphs of text) and images (multiple animations). What can you do?

Several studies suggest you should offload information to the verbal channel. Ideally, you'd be able to watch the animation and have that be your only visual input. If instead of also reading paragraphs of text, you listened to someone narrate the same information while you watched the animation (think how-to video), you would be less likely to experience cognitive overload.

The amount of information in each scenario is identical. However, splitting it across the visual and verbal channels means neither is flooded to the point where thinking breaks down.

1 The dual-channel assumption is part of both Paivio's dual-coding theory and Baddeley's theory of working memory. While scholars of each do not characterize the subsystems exactly the same way, the differences may be more interesting to graduate psychology students than readers of this book. In this chapter, we'll highlight what they have in common and what's been learned across the two bodies of research.

In the last chapter we talked about trimming unnecessary content to lighten the burden on working memory. That wouldn't have worked here. Learners need to see the parts of the toilet and they need to learn what each does and in what order. There's no extraneous information to cut. That's why taking advantage of our two pathways for processing information (visual and verbal) is so important. You get around the limits of working memory by dividing the same amount of information across two channels.

You can also lighten the load by signaling to learners what is most important to pay attention to. These cues can be visual (arrows, bolding, color coding, circling, and other annotations) and verbal ("There are three things you need to do. First..."). This reduces cognitive load because rather than using mental resources to search for what's worth attending to, learners can focus on making sense of key ideas.

Boost Retention

As an added bonus, taking advantage of our two channels for processing information doesn't just help you avoid overload. It also boosts your retention of the information. Dual coding theory suggests we have better retention when images and words are combined because it gives us two ways to remember the information.

Here's an example. Think about someone who has just moved and is getting familiar with their new neighborhood. During their second time heading to the store, they might repeat to themselves, "Remember, right on East Parkway, left on Poplar Avenue, left into the parking lot." They may also recall certain visual cues, which remind them where to turn. Or they may picture the route in their mind and use that to navigate. By utilizing both channels – verbal (directions) and visual (picturing the route) – they have multiple ways to remember how to get to the store.

In addition, researchers have noted it takes a *lot* of verbal information (enough to cause cognitive overload) to provide the same level of detail that is contained in most images. Because of this, images are often a more efficient way to recall information.

We don't want to be misleading. Researchers have found that it's possible for learners to recall information that was presented in a single channel (e.g. a text-only article). They have also found participants can recall information when it was presented one channel at a time (e.g. read an article, then look at the accompanying image). However, in several experiments, cognitive scientists have shown that learners who were exposed to the same information through both channels concurrently (e.g. narration over animation) had:

- The basic recall of peers in the study who were presented with information through one channel at a time.
- Significantly higher scores on problem solving and transfer tasks (e.g. using information from a "how it works" video to figure out how to repair a toilet) than control groups.

The takeaway? If you want to improve recall and transfer, take advantage of both the verbal and visual channels.

Research-Based Dos and Don'ts

Here's a list of four strategies that experiments have shown are effective ways to open up space for relevant processing. They use what we know about dual-channel processing to reduce unnecessary cognitive load. The list also includes strategies that help you take advantage of the verbal and visual channels to boost retention and transfer.

Don't Make People Listen to You Read Slides

- **Don't:** Have you ever attended a presentation where someone reads the text they have on a slide? This forces learners to engage in unnecessary processing as they try to sync what they are reading to what the presenter is saying.
- **Instead:** Show an image or key takeaway; narrate the rest.

Don't Ask People to Hold Information in One Channel in Order to Make Sense of Something in the Other

- **Don't:** If you show an animation of how a toilet works and then have learners read text describing the process, they have to hold the series of images in working memory, while also trying to map the text onto them.
- **Don't:** The reverse is also a problem. If they read the information first, then while they watch the animation they have to try to recall what they read.
- **Instead:**
    - Reduce unnecessary processing by presenting information concurrently (e.g. narrating over animation). This gives learners exactly what they need, when they need it.
    - When you see a long block of text, ask yourself, "Is there a way to turn this into a table, process, or diagram?" Adding a visual component, even by just converting text into a table with clear headers, means you'll reap the memory benefits of using visuals

and text. Minimizing text means you can do this without flooding the verbal channel.

Do Signal What Is Important

- **Do:** Make the most of the visual channel by using arrows, bolding, intentional color coding, and other annotations to direct learners' attention. This signals to learners where to look, what's important, and how information is related. Verbal channel examples might include cues like "First," "Step 1" or "The most important thing is...".
- **Do:** Put labels right next to the relevant part of a diagram rather than bury key information in a paragraph on another part of the page.
- **Why:** This helps make sure learners aren't wasting valuable working memory space trying to figure out where to look, what's related, or what's important.

Do Prompt Learners to Use Both Channels (Verbal and Visual), Even If You Are Constrained to One

Sometimes you are constrained to audio or text only and you can't present through both channels concurrently (hello, this book! We'd love to be narrating over well-crafted animations, but we can't do that on the printed page).

You can still prompt learners to activate both channels:

- **Do:** Use concrete examples or analogies that are easy to visualize. Ask learners to imagine what something looks like or bring to mind an associated image. For example, "Imagine the roots of a tree."
- **Why:** The visual they create in their mind becomes a way to recall the information in the future.
- **Do:** Prompt referential connections. If you are presenting words and images, ask learners to explain how the text and images are related. Make sure they get specific. For example, "Which sections of the text relate to which sections of the diagram?"
- **Why:** Referential connections (relating words to images) are associated not just with recall but with problem solving and transfer.

How can you use what you know about the dual-channel assumption to effectively communicate? For that we'll turn to our next mental model.

Two Ways to Process Information in Practice

Big Idea: Get around the limits of working memory and boost retention by taking advantage of both channels for processing information: Verbal and visual.

Mental Model: Channel Your Inner Meteorologist.

To get around the limits of working memory and boost retention, channel your inner meteorologist by doing these two things:

- **Narrate over your weather map:** Take advantage of both channels (verbal and visual) by narrating over images.
- **Mark up your weather map:** Point out key information along the way.

Here's what we mean.

Step 1: Narrate Over Your Weather Map

This step calls on you to take advantage of both channels (verbal and visual) by narrating over images. Think about when you watch a weather segment on your local news channel. The news station doesn't ask you to read a bunch of text about the forecast while also looking at an animated map. The weather presenter narrates over the map, describing the movement of weather patterns as they happen. Do the same thing when you are presenting information.

In case you aren't working for the local news station, let's look at what Channel Your Inner Meteorologist might look like in another context. Imagine a colleague has been tasked with synthesizing client feedback on an older product that has very low user engagement. They have to present the feedback to their team and share a draft of their presentation with you for feedback first. Using what you know about dual-channel processing, you suggest the following changes.

What they sent you...

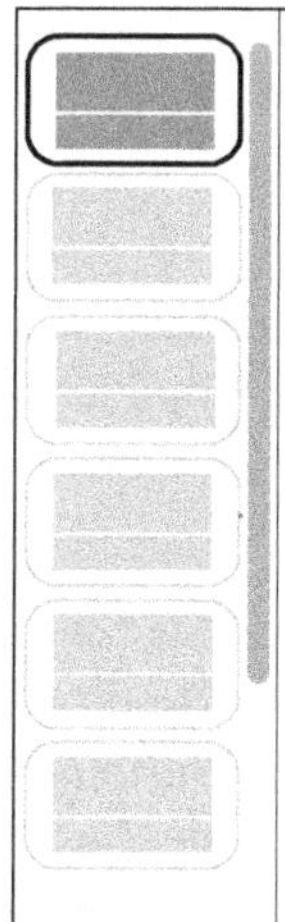

Users are experiencing several pain points.

- When they try to search, most of the results that come up are not tightly related to their search terms.
- Clients regularly search for content that we say we focus on and there are no relevant results.

Your suggestions

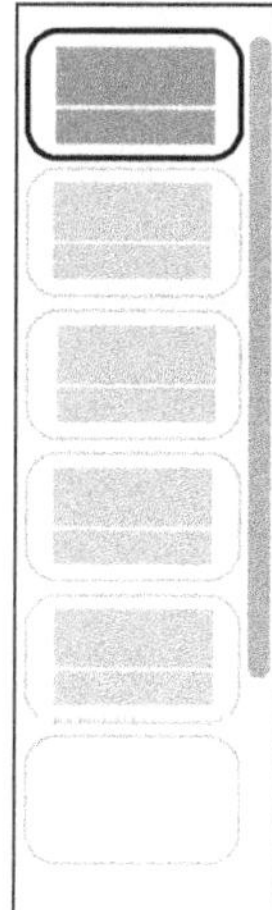

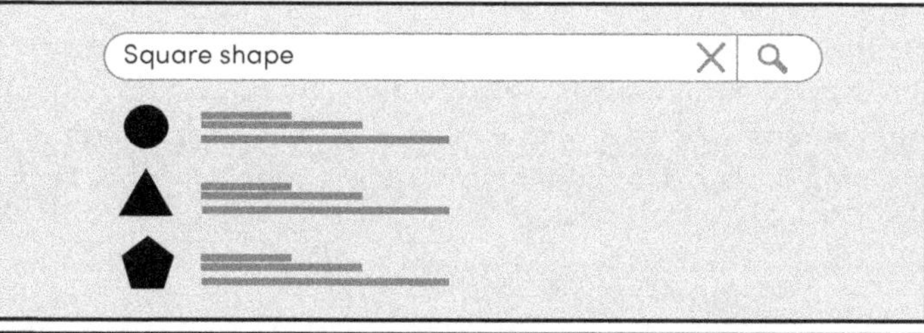

Users are experiencing several pain points. For example, When they try to search, most of the results that come up are not tightly related to their search terms.

Clients regularly search for content that we say we focus on and there are no relevant results.

Why these changes? While your colleague did a great job of not cluttering the slide with text, it's on the listener to imagine what each of the issues looks like. While they do that, the image on the screen is competing for space in the visual channel.

Chunking the content across multiple slides and syncing the images to exactly match what the speaker is describing when they describe it will reduce the chances of cognitive overload. It will also prompt referential connections between the images and client feedback. Circling specific results is also an example of pointing out key information, which takes us to step 2.

Step 2: Mark Up Your Weather Map

This step requires you to point out key information as you go. When a meteorologist presents the weather on the news, they gesture with their hands to show you where to focus your attention. They also use color coding to help you make sense of information. For example, they may point out the most intense part of the storm as it moves across the map by coloring it dark red. When there's a lot to take in at once, they'll use titles, labels, or arrows, or they might even circle the most important thing to attend to.

Bring that spirit to your presentations and writing. Bold key words. Use arrows, color coding, and labels to help learners know what to pay attention to and what it means. Don't go wild with your annotations, though. Too many will be distracting and add to, rather than lighten, cognitive load. Only highlight what is most important.

Here's how you might support your colleague with this.

What they sent you...

When I opened this I thought this just looks and feels so dated. Why would I trust this information when it so clearly hasn't been touched for years? I saw this and within 30 seconds said, "No thanks." I'm a busy person. Why use something that might waste my time?

- Darren

Read quote on the screen:
When I opened this I thought this just looks and feels so dated. Why would I trust this information when it so clearly hasn't been touched for years? I saw this and within 30 seconds said, "No thanks." I'm a busy person. Why use something that might waste my time? - Darren

Your suggestions

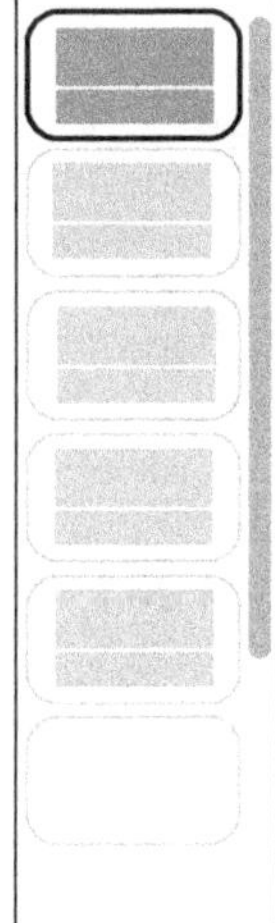

When I opened this I thought this just looks and feels so dated. **Why would I trust this information when it so clearly hasn't been touched for years?** I saw this and within 30 seconds said, "No thanks." I'm a busy person. Why use something that might waste my time?

- Darren

In a moment, you'll see a quote from one of our clients on the screen. I'll give you a second to read that.

These changes help in two ways. First, you spare listeners from having to do a bunch of extra processing as they try to sync what they are reading on the slide to what the presenter is saying. Second, in terms of "mark up the map," bolding helps signal what is important. Working memory is used for processing what that means, rather than "What are they hoping I take away from this?"

Take It Further: Map the Connections

These steps help you avoid cognitive overload and promote retention. But you can take this a step further. Adding in opportunities to create referential connections between visuals and information supports transfer.

We've already mentioned that concurrent narration and animation is one way to help learners build referential connections. What they hear matches what they are seeing in real time. Therefore, they know which parts of the information relate to which part of the image. If you don't have the luxury of narration over animation, you can still promote these connections. This might sound like saying to attendees, "This is a quote from a focus group. What stands out to you about what he raises, especially in relation to the issues you saw on the previous slides?"

Of course, these aren't the only ways this presentation could be improved. Across these examples what we hope you take away is that channeling your inner meteorologist can help you communicate more effectively.

Conclusion

All of us want to avoid cognitive overload. However, we often fall into the trap of assuming that the only way to do this is to cut information. While this is an important skill, it's equally important to consider how we can spread information across our verbal and visual channels.

Takeaways

Understanding we use two channels (verbal and visual) for processing information matters because:

- You'll know how to reduce the burden on working memory in one channel by offloading information to the other.
- You'll signal to learners what to pay attention to in the visual channel – bolding, circling, and color coding – so they don't waste valuable working memory space trying to figure out what matters.
- You'll know that there's an added bonus:
    - Presenting information in both channels boosts retention because learners will have two ways to remember the information.
    - Prompting connections between images and information boosts problem solving and transfer.

References and further reading

Baddeley, A. (1998). *Human Memory.* Boston: Allyn & Bacon.

Clark, J. M., & Paivio, A. (1991). Dual coding theory and education. *Educational Psychology Review, 3,* 149–210.

Dunlosky, J., Rawson, K. A., Marsh, E. J., Nathan, M. J., & Willingham, D. T. (2013). Improving students' learning with effective learning techniques: Promising directions from cognitive and educational psychology. *Psychological Science in the Public interest, 14*(1), 4–58.

Mayer, R. E. (2001). *Multimedia Learning.* New York: Cambridge University Press.

Mayer, R. E., & Anderson, R. B. (1992). The instructive animation: Helping students build connections between words and pictures in multimedia learning. *Journal of Educational Psychology, 84*(4), 444–452.

Mayer, R. E., & Moreno, R. (2003). Nine ways to reduce cognitive load in multimedia learning. *Educational Psychologist, 38*(1), 43–52.

Mayer, R. E., & Sims, V. K. (1994). For whom is a picture worth a thousand words? Extensions of a dual-coding theory of multimedia learning. *Journal of Educational Psychology, 86*(3), 389–401.

Meilinger, T., Knauff, M., & Bülthoff, H. H. (2008). Working memory in wayfinding – A dual task experiment in a virtual city. *Cognitive Science, 32*(4), 755–770.

Paivio, A. (1986). *Mental representations: A dual coding approach.* Oxford, England: Oxford University Press

Sadoski, M., & Paivio, A. (2004). A dual coding theoretical model of reading. In R. B. Ruddell & N. J. Unrau (eds.) *Theoretical Models and Processes of Reading* (5th ed.), Newark, DE: International Reading Association, pp. 1329–1362.

Smith, M, & Weinstein, Y. (2019). *Learn how to study using... dual coding.* The Learning Scientists. Available at: www.learningscientists.org/blog/2016/9/1-1 (Accessed: December 12, 2024).

Ward, M., & Sweller, J. (1990). Structuring effective worked examples. *Cognition and Instruction, 7*(1), 1–39.

11. RECIPES FOR SUCCESS: USE WORKED EXAMPLES TO DRIVE NEW LEARNING

Instructional manuals have been around for a long time. Probably because, for centuries, people have had to complete tasks for which they have no idea where to begin.

In the 3rd or 4th century, Graeco-Egyptian alchemist Zosimus of Panopolis believed alchemical knowledge – the quest to transform base metals into gold – should be public. He created a manual full of recipes and how-to guides that were reputedly passed down by fallen angels.

In the Middle Ages, pocket-sized manuals on topics like how to perform surgery became popular. They were referred to as "vade mecum," which literally means "go with me" in Latin. While it's great that these manuals increased access to important knowledge, watching your surgeon fish in their pocket for a step-by-step guide of how to perform your operation could not have inspired much confidence.

After the advent of the printing press, manuals proliferated. In 1683, Joseph Maxim printed the *Mechanick Exercises,* a book that taught others how to use the printing press. Manuals like this democratized access to professions. For the first time you could learn to do something without being a part of a guild or completing an apprenticeship.

Cognitive scientists call the step-by-step, illustrated solutions that are so often found in user manuals "worked examples," and there's a reason they've been around so long. Worked examples are one of the most effective ways to help someone do something they've never done before. There is, of course, a cognition-based reason for this. And thankfully, we have decades of research rather than just the word of fallen angels to help us understand why.

Worked Examples

At their most basic, worked examples show a solution to a problem. Let's take a look at this through the example of a topic you are familiar with: Multiplication. This is often introduced in second or third grade. If you were introducing it to elementary schoolers for the first time, you might show the worked example below.

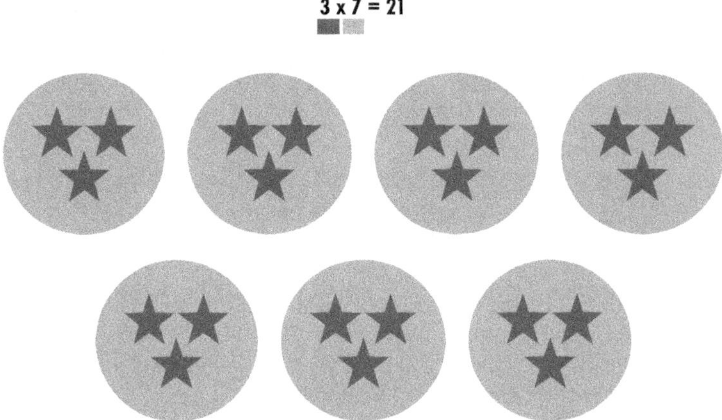

While this may seem intuitive to most, notice what is happening here. This is an effective worked example because it shows the solution (21) and the path to get there (seven equal groups of three). This obviously isn't the only worked example you could show. You could also show students an addition sentence such as 3 + 3 + 3 + 3 + 3 + 3 + 3.

Like this example, many worked examples include diagrams and other annotations. For example, think of the pictures in the instructions you used the last time you had to assemble furniture.

Some worked examples contain procedural step-by-step instructions, but this isn't required. For example, in 2013 when Kyun and colleagues provided participants with a writing prompt paired with an exemplar essay (no annotations or step-by-step instructions) they were still able to effectively boost participants' writing skills. So whether there are visuals, annotations, step-by-step instructions, or none of these things, what's key is that readers see an accurate solution and ideally a clear path to get there.

Across a variety of domains, such math, physics, computer programming, mechanics, and writing, researchers have found that worked examples lead to increased effectiveness. Beginning with Sweller and Cooper's 1985 study of worked examples, experiments for several decades show that studying worked examples is an efficient way to learn new things. When novices study worked examples, they are able to learn to solve similar problems independently, in less time, compared to groups who just went straight to practice after initial instruction. Learners who studied worked examples also made fewer errors in their independent work.

So, cognitively speaking, how do worked examples help? You learned in chapter 2 that we remember concrete examples easier than abstract theories. That's part of what makes worked examples so powerful. They don't just provide a series of steps in a procedure; they provide learners with a concrete example of what it looks like to actually carry those out to solve a real problem.

But that's not the only reason worked examples are helpful. When you are trying to do something brand new, you have to figure out a few things, including what type of problem you are looking at and what's the best way to solve it. Worked examples make this a lot easier.

Take the multiplication example we showed you earlier. If you're a third-grader and it's your first time seeing 3 × 7, you have to figure out that this is a multiplication problem and what that means (you are finding the total from equal groups). You also have to identify a strategy you can reliably use to do that (count by threes, seven times). Even after you figure all that out, you still have to successfully complete each step to solve it (count by threes, without errors). That's a tall order for an 8-year-old because it is a lot to hold in your mind at once. For novices, it often leads to cognitive overload.

With worked examples, rather than the learner searching the problem space for a strategy that might work ("Should I draw a diagram? Add?"), the solution steps are provided. This opens up working memory space for understanding each step and how it helps you get to a solution successfully (e.g. "Why did they draw three stars in each circle?").

With worked examples, the learner's focus switches from problem solving ("How do I solve this problem?") to *learning* ("How does this work? How might this strategy help me solve problems like this in the future?"). Put in the language of cognitive science, the learner is studying each component of a specific solution and storing it in long-term memory. They do this so that they can retrieve them later when they see it might be useful.

Obviously, worked examples won't teach the learner everything they need to know about a certain topic. Once a learner can solve a problem without the support of the worked example, you'll want to begin integrating other problem types. This way they practice identifying what type of problem they are looking at and determining the best way to solve it. So while we acknowledge that worked examples are not a silver bullet (is anything?), we want to stamp that they *are* one of the most efficient ways to help someone add a new strategy to their toolkit.

The Illusion of Understanding

Despite all the benefits of worked examples, people aren't great at using them. How many times have you opened the box for a new item, glanced at the instructions and thought, "Easy," and then as you attempted to use it said, "Wait, what?"

To understand this better, in 1997 researcher Alexander Renkl looked at participants who learned from worked examples (effective users) and those who didn't (ineffective users). He asked participants to describe what they were thinking as they looked at the worked examples so he could learn more about learners' processes.

When researchers listened to learners describe their thinking as they looked at the worked examples, they found two types of ineffective users: Passive explainers and superficial explainers.

- **Passive explainers** had extremely low levels of description. To put it plainly, researchers realized this group was not doing much thinking about the worked examples as they looked at them.
- **Superficial explainers** shared more thoughts. However, compared to the successful learners, they spent little time on each example. They moved quickly through the set without taking time to make sure they deeply understood each strategy.

It's important to know that most people in the study were ineffective users. Subsequent studies have shown that like the passive and superficial explainers, most people who look at worked examples delude themselves. Instead of engaging in the deep processing that would help them store information in long-term memory, they give those step-by-step instructions in a car manual a quick glance, and think, "Got it."

And in study after study, it turned out they do not, in fact, get it. Cognitive scientists call this the "illusion of understanding." Under this illusion, learners report feelings of understanding when they look at worked examples but aren't able to solve problems on their own.

There's something extremely relatable in this phenomenon. Together, several studies point to the fact that many people (including us) need support if they are to learn from worked examples. Luckily, researchers have homed in on a few methods that are particularly helpful.

Making the Most of Worked Examples

Let's return to Renkl's study of effective and ineffective users of worked examples. What were the effective users doing that was so useful? Effective users tended to engage in two types of reasoning: Meaning-focused reasoning and anticipative reasoning.

- **Meaning-focused reasoning** assigns, you guessed it, meaning to each step of a process. In our multiplication example that might sound like the learner saying "The seven shows how many equal groups there are. The three shows how many objects are in each group." The learner assigns meaning to each number.
- **Anticipative reasoning** occurs when a learner predicts the next step of a solution. Normally they use this as a way to check their understanding. For example: "Okay, so next step, I need to find the total. I'll count by threes seven times: 3, 6, 9, 12, 15, 18, 21. Yes, that's what they got! The total is 21."

Self-Explanation

To get people to engage in more meaning-focused reasoning, Renkl and several of his colleagues started prompting learners to engage in what they called "self-explanation." These prompts ask learners to explain the purpose of each step ("Why are there three stars in each circle?") or identify principles that sit under each step of a process.

Why does this help? These prompts increase the quality of learners' thinking as they engage with worked examples in a few ways. They direct learners' attention to what is most important about the worked example – what the steps to arrive at a solution are and why they are used in this context.

These prompts also force learners to engage in deep processing. As you know from earlier chapters, this makes learners more likely to remember the information later. In addition, they help learners integrate what they are seeing in the worked example with what they already know.

It's worth the time to add these prompts. In several experiments, with content ranging from algebra to argumentation, Renkl and his colleagues have found that when learners are prompted to engage in self-explanation as they look at worked examples, they learn more than peers who don't have access to the prompts. Specifically, learners do better on measures of basic recall, domain knowledge, near transfer (different surface features but same deep structure) and far transfer (different surface features and different deep structure). In other words, they learn more *and* they are able to use what they learn from the worked examples to complete new tasks independently.

Fading

Researchers also wanted a way to prompt learners to engage in the anticipative reasoning of successful learners from worked examples. To do this, they started "fading" worked examples.

Here's what that might look like:

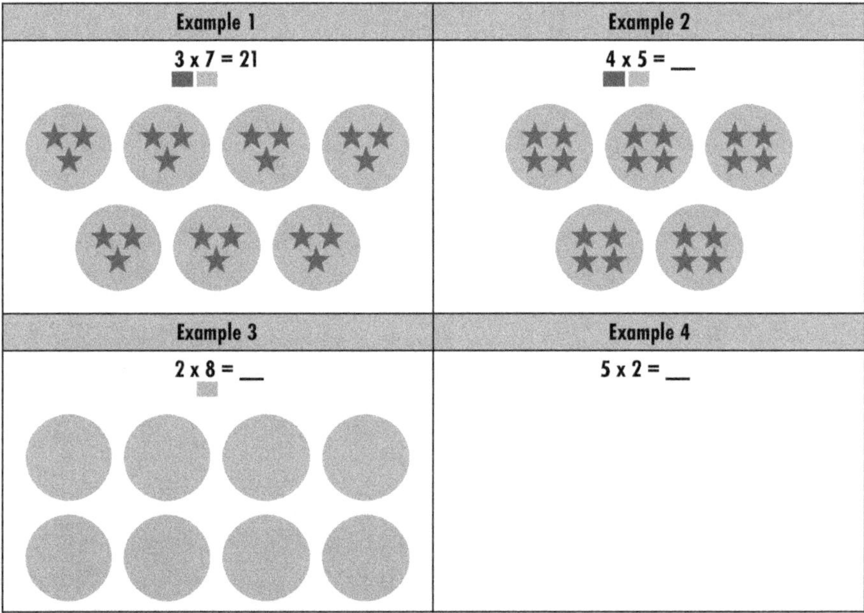

In faded worked examples, one step is removed at a time until the learner is completing the entire problem on their own.

Why is fading helpful? First, it prompts active processing of the worked example. You can't be a passive explainer if you are required to complete parts of the problem yourself. You are forced to engage in that useful anticipative reasoning; you have to identify what should happen next and complete the step yourself.

It also functions as a type of what cognitive scientists call "retrieval practice." To complete faded worked examples, you have to "retrieve" the next step from long-term memory. Every time you do this, it strengthens the memory trace.

Fading also follows models of cognitive apprenticeship. The gradual release of responsibility from the complete example to the learner adjusts the difficulty of the task to the growing background knowledge of the learner. This ensures the right balance of support and autonomy as learners engage with new information.

Evidence suggests fading worked examples is a powerful strategy. In a 2003 study by Atkinson and colleagues, learners who studied faded worked examples were able to successfully solve more problems on near-transfer tasks than learners who studied non-faded worked examples. They also (unsurprisingly) outperformed peers who didn't have access to worked examples.

Researchers have found a few other important things about fading. Order matters. It's more effective to fade backward, as in the faded multiplication examples above. If you track the progression, you'll see we left off the last step (the solution), then the second to last step (the number of objects in each circle), etc. Studies have shown this is more effective than fading in the opposite direction, where learners encounter an example that's missing the first step.

If you can combine fading and self-explanation ("How did you know how many stars to draw in each circle?"), even better. Atkinson and colleagues found large effects on near *and* far transfer tasks when fading was combined with prompts for self-explanation like those described in the earlier section.

A Few Other Tips

You've heard this in earlier chapters, but feedback matters. You can prompt a learner to engage in self-explanation or anticipative reasoning, but if their responses are incorrect and they never receive information otherwise, it's not going to be very helpful. Actually, it's worse. They are practicing the wrong thing. This means inaccurate information will be stored in long-term memory.

Find a way to both prompt active processing through self-explanation and fading *and* give your learner feedback. You could:

- Provide them with real-time feedback on the accuracy of their responses.
- Have them select the next step or underlying principle from a preset list (e.g. "This number shows a) the number of equal groups, b) the number inside each equal group, or c) the total"). Immediately show them whether the option they chose was correct. Let them revise if it's incorrect.
- Have them answer the question independently. After they respond, give them an exemplar that they can compare their answer to.

All of these help a learner know whether they are understanding the worked example and internalizing the information accurately. Put another way, it helps them avoid the "illusion of understanding" and ensure they are actually learning from the worked examples.

Another thing to keep in mind – some worked examples are more effective than others. In the previous chapter, we discussed how researchers have found it's essential to integrate annotations within accompanying diagrams so as not to cause the split-attention effect. Make sure you aren't unnecessarily adding to your learners' cognitive load by making them constantly switch attention between text and accompanying visuals in a solution.

Finally, worked examples are ideal for people who are learning something new. Researchers have found something called the expertise reversal effect. As you now know, novices learn more efficiently when they have the opportunity to study worked examples before they solve problems independently. The more of a novice you are with the material, the more this helps. Experts, on the other hand, benefit more from being able to jump right into solving problems in their domain of expertise, rather than studying worked examples. If you already know how to multiply, studying the worked example above is unlikely to add anything to your schema. In fact, taking time to study it may unnecessarily add to your working memory load.

Worked Examples in Practice

Big Idea: Avoid cognitive overload by supporting learners with worked examples when you ask them to try something new.

Mental Model: The Baking Show.

If you want to help someone new to a topic learn how to do something, drawing from the format of your favorite baking show is a great place to start.

Tip 1: Give Them a Recipe by Sharing a Worked Example

Just like a worked example, a recipe provides step-by-step instructions. While expert bakers can bake without a recipe, put their own twist on a classic, or even invent their own creations, recipes are key for novices. If you ever baked, you know the best recipes don't just tell you what to do. They also tell you what you should look for and what you'll hear and smell, and they will give you notes on taste and texture for various components.

Here's what this might look like. Imagine there's a restructure at your organization and someone you manage is being asked to absorb new workstreams. One of her new tasks is going to be to write a blog post each week. In a one-on-one, she shares that she's nervous because she's never written one before.

If you were "giving her a recipe," you might:

1. Grab an existing blog post that exemplifies the type of writing you want her to emulate (e.g. a post that has generated great engagement, a post that shows a new format the organization wants to use, or whatever it is you want her to do). This will be her worked example.
2. Annotate it to call out the "ingredients" you want her to use as she writes her first post. For example, you might underline and label the following "ingredients."
    a. Hook: Anecdote, real example, data, quote.
    b. Topic sentence: Clear statement of the big idea.
    c. Explanation: A few sentences expanding on the big idea with at least one concrete example.
    d. Call to action: A strategy for readers to try out on their own and a link to a downloadable resource with email capture.

Tip 2: Interview Them as They Work by Prompting Self-Explanation

Footage of the host circulating and asking contestants to explain what they are doing is a staple of most baking shows. Their interview questions (e.g. "Why'd you do that?" "So after you have this all mixed, what's next?") are actually remarkably similar to the prompts for self-explanation that cognitive scientists have found to boost understanding. Use this pillar of most baking shows the next time you support someone with worked examples.

In our example, this might mean setting up a time with your colleague to talk through the annotated blog post you sent. In the meeting, you might say something like "I sent over a post marked up with some key ingredients I'll ask you to include in each of your posts. Walk me through what you see as the purpose of each and we can talk through any questions you have." This will prompt her to engage in self-explanation and increase the likelihood she internalizes each step.

Tip 3: Challenge Them with Unfinished Recipes Using Fading

In one well-known baking show, there is a technical challenge in each episode. During this segment contestants receive partial instructions or an unfinished recipe. They have to use what they know to fill in the rest. The judges taste their final products and determine who came closest to the goal.

An unfinished recipe is actually a great example of fading. After learners have had a chance to study a full worked example, fade out support, one step at a time. Remember, order matters. Fade out the last step, second to last, and so on – not the other way around.

What does this look like with your colleague? After you meet, send her a few exercises to work through on her own over the course of a week as part of her onboarding to her new workstream. You could pull four more existing blog posts with the steps faded out back to front. In the first post, leave off the strategy and downloadable resource section. Ask her to complete the post and then compare her version to the published post.

Repeat the step above with a new post, but this time just give the hook and big idea and leave off the rest. Keep fading until she's producing the post in its entirety. By this point, she'll be able to churn out high-quality posts, quickly and independently.

A Final Note

In the examples above, we describe using worked examples to support someone else in learning something new. However, worked examples are also one of the most efficient ways you can teach *yourself* a new skill.

For example, when Rebekah was in grad school, she wanted to improve her ability to write research articles – specifically the introduction and literature reviews. She would take seminal articles in her field and use them as worked examples. She'd annotate them, labeling the purpose of each paragraph (self-explanation). Sadly, she didn't think to incorporate fading. Even so, she began to notice that across the papers, there seemed to be a few common ways authors opened their articles and structured their literature reviews. She began using them herself and her writing improved.

Conclusion

As adults, there are lots of things we need to learn quickly. We won't always have the opportunity to take a course, attend a training, or have someone teach us. In these instances, rather than just saying, "Here goes nothing," set yourself up for success finding your own worked examples. You'll avoid cognitive overload, and your final product will be better. Better yet, if you study them effectively, you'll have added new skills to your toolbelt that will last for the long run.

Takeaways

- Avoid overload. Worked examples lighten cognitive load in a productive way – they open up space for novices to focus on learning a new strategy rather than just make sense of the problem at hand.
- Worked examples are a great strategy to use with novices. For people who already have expertise, studying worked examples is unnecessary.
- Supercharge your support. Adding prompts for self-explanation and fading support one step at a time makes worked examples even more powerful.

References and further reading

Atkinson, R. K., & Renkl, A. (2007). Interactive example-based learning environments: Using interactive elements to encourage effective processing of worked examples. *Educational Psychology Review, 19*, 375–386.

Atkinson, R. K., Renkl, A., & Merrill, M. M. (2003). Transitioning from studying examples to solving problems: Effects of self-explanation prompts and fading worked-out steps. *Journal of Educational Psychology, 95*(4), 774–783.

Bokosmaty, S., Sweller, J., & Kalyuga, S. (2015). Learning geometry problem solving by studying worked examples: Effects of learner guidance and expertise. *American Educational Research Journal, 52*(2), 307–333.

Creager, A. N. H., Grote, M., & Leong, E. (2020). Learning by the book: Manuals and handbooks in the history of science. *BJHS Themes, 5*, 1–13.

Dunlosky, J., Rawson, K. A., Marsh, E. J., Nathan, M. J., & Willingham, D. T. (2013). Improving students' learning with effective learning techniques: Promising directions from cognitive and educational psychology. *Psychological Science in the Public interest, 14*(1), 4–58.

Hilbert, T. S., Schworm, S., & Renkl, A. (2004). Learning from worked-out examples: The transition from instructional explanations to self-explanation prompts. *Instructional Design for Effective and Enjoyable Computer-Supported Learning*, 184–192.

Kalyuga, S., Chandler, P., Tuovinen, J., & Sweller, J. (2001). When problem solving is superior to studying worked examples. *Journal of Educational Psychology, 93*(3), 579–588.

Kyun, S., Kalyuga, S., & Sweller, J. (2013). The effect of worked examples when learning to write essays in English literature. *The Journal of Experimental Education, 81*(3), 385–408.

Moxon, J. (1683). *Mechanick exercises, or, The doctrine of handy-works: applied to the art of printing: the second volumne.* Internet Archive. Available at: https://archive.org/details/mechanickexercis00moxo_0/page/n448/mode/1up (Accessed: December 13, 2024).

Paas, F., Renkl, A., & Sweller, J. (2003). Cognitive load theory and instructional design: Recent developments. *Educational Psychologist, 38*(1), 1–4.

Renkl, A. (1997). Learning from worked-out examples: A study on individual differences. *Cognitive Science, 21*(1), 1–29.

Renkl, A. (1999). Learning mathematics from worked-out examples: Analyzing and fostering self-explanations. *European Journal of Psychology of Education, 14*(4), 477–488.

Renkl, A. (2002). Worked-out examples: Instructional explanations support learning by self-explanations. *Learning and Instruction, 12*(5), 529–556.

Salden, R. J., Koedinger, K. R., Renkl, A., Aleven, V., & McLaren, B. M. (2010). Accounting for beneficial effects of worked examples in tutored problem solving. *Educational Psychology Review, 22*, 379–392.

Schumacher, H. (2022). *Inside the world of instruction manuals.* BBC Future. www.bbc.com/future/article/20180403-inside-the-world-of-instruction-manuals (Accessed: December 12, 2024).

Schworm, S., & Renkl, A. (2007). Learning argumentation skills through the use of prompts for self-explaining examples. *Journal of Educational Psychology, 99*(2), 285–296.

Svenvold, M. (2015). *The disappearance of the instruction manual.* Popular Science. Available at: www.popsci.com/instructions-not-included/ (Accessed: December 13, 2024).

Sweller, J., & Cooper, G. A. (1985). The use of worked examples as a substitute for problem solving in learning algebra. *Cognition and Instruction, 2*(1), 59–89.

Tuovinen, J. E., & Sweller, J. (1999). A comparison of cognitive load associated with discovery learning and worked examples. *Journal of Educational Psychology, 91*(2), 334–341.

vade mecum. (n.d.). In *Merriam-Webster Dictionary.* Available at: www.merriam-webster.com/dictionary/vade%20mecum

van Gog, T., Kester, L., & Paas, F. (2011). Effects of worked examples, example-problem, and problem-example pairs on novices' learning. *Contemporary Educational Psychology, 36*(3), 212–218.

van Merriënboer, J. J., Kirschner, P. A., & Kester, L. (2003). Taking the load off a learner's mind: Instructional design for complex learning. *Educational Psychologist, 38*(1), 5–13.

Ward, M., & Sweller, J. (1990). Structuring effective worked examples. *Cognition and Instruction, 7*(1), 1–39.

Zosimus. (2018). In *Cambridge University Press eBooks* (pp. 196–201). https://doi.org/10.1017/9781316856567.012

12. SEE WHAT I DID THERE?: MODEL TO QUICKLY BUILD EXPERTISE

> "My Reverend Father, the visits that I have made from time to time at Jingdezhen ... have given me in turn an opportunity to instruct myself concerning the manner in which one makes this beautiful porcelain which is so admired and which is exported to all parts of the world ... I believe that a detailed description of all that is concerned with this sort of work should be of some use in Europe."

So begins a letter from Father Francois Xavier d'Entrecolles, a Jesuit missionary who was sent to China during the height of the French court's obsession with porcelain for the explicit purpose of stealing the secrets of making it. His letters from Jingdezhen, the city most renowned for its porcelain work, included information on necessary ingredients and the process for turning them into porcelain. They also included advanced techniques for glazing, firing, and aging. His letters were so detailed that Josiah Wedgwood (yes, that Wedgwood) later used them to recreate the Jingdezhen assembly lines in his factory.

It shouldn't come as a surprise that expertise is rare, and people will go to great (and illegal) lengths to get it. And unfortunately, Father Francois isn't the only one.

Governments have passed policies to prevent this type of behavior for a long time. The earliest known recognition of intellectual property rights is from 500 BCE where chefs in the Mediterranean city Sybaris became concerned rivals were stealing their recipes. As a result, city leaders decided to grant chefs exclusive ownership of their recipes for one year.

Fast forward to the 1700s, corporate espionage was such a problem that the British made passing on trade secrets punishable by death. This didn't stop people like Samuel Slater from copying plans for a water-powered mill or Francis Lowell from recreating the mill from memory and bringing them back to New England for extraordinary economic gain.

Today, intellectual property rights can still be highly litigious. The stakes are high because knowledge is so valuable. But let's imagine for a moment that this wasn't the case. Imagine organizations and people sharing their intellectual property freely. Problem solved, right? Unfortunately, no.

As you may recall from chapter 2, experts are often incredibly ineffective at sharing what they know. This "curse of expertise" refers to a pervasive cognitive bias where we assume that others have the same level of background information we do. The more expertise you have, the harder time you have explaining the basics to someone who is new to the content.

The takeaway? Don't assume that just because you have expertise, you'll be able to explain something. You actually may be less effective than someone with less background knowledge.

If you want to share your expertise, one of the most effective ways is to engage in modeling and think-alouds. Rather than making ham-fisted attempts to explain concepts, experts use these tools to show rather than tell. We'll explore what effective modeling looks like and how it supports learning in the rest of this chapter.

What is Modeling?

Modeling is when you demonstrate, in real time, how to do something. You've probably done this lots of times. Remember when you showed your sibling how to do laundry? That was modeling.

Modeling is a highly effective way to help someone learn something new. Decades of experiments show that it helps people efficiently acquire new skills and increase performance across a variety of contexts including classrooms, industrial work, people management, medical training, social skills, and sports. These results are consistent whether people watch someone model how to do something in person or on video.

And that's not all. In 2002, Pedersen and Liu also found that when they give people identical information – in one condition through modeling (someone performing a task) and in another by sharing all of the same information provided in the modeling condition, but without expert modeling – people learn more from modeling. It's also important to note that the things that people learn from modeling are likely to stick. A meta-analysis by Taylor and colleagues of 117 studies in workplace settings show that exposure to modeling is related to increased knowledge (immediately) and job performance (over time).

When researchers first began studying modeling, some scholars were concerned that it promoted mimicry, not learning. Imagine someone watching a presenter model how to introduce themselves to a stranger by saying, "What a beautiful day! I'm Priscilla, by the way." Scholars were concerned that learners would parrot this phrasing inflexibly, whether on a sunny day or in the midst of a tornado. Researchers quickly put this to rest by checking whether watching someone model a skill supported performance on the same task – where you could technically get away with repeating what you heard – as well as on different, related tasks where mimicry wouldn't help. In study after study, it boosted performance on both identical and different tasks. In other words, modeling supports transfer.

The benefits of modeling aren't limited to skill acquisition. After watching someone model how to do something, learners report higher self-efficacy (or belief that they can succeed with the task) and demonstrate greater self-regulation. They also report greater interest in the task and increased positive feelings about the learning environment. Taken together, these studies make a strong case for using modeling as a way to teach something new.

Access to Expertise

It might be tempting to say we are all benefiting from modeling almost all the time. All we have to do is observe the people around us. You could watch your partner flip a pancake, neighborhood kids play basketball, or your coworker give a presentation. But just because people are engaging in observable behavior doesn't mean that they are modeling. This is for a few reasons.

First, modeling is generally more effective when it's done by someone with some degree of expertise. Your 4-year-old is going to learn how to write the letter 'A' faster from an adult who has mastered the skill than from a fellow preschooler who is also learning it for the first time. As we raised in the introduction with the "curse of expertise" this, of course, isn't a given. It's true if, and only if, the expert knows how to model effectively.

Second, effective modeling is not just doing something while someone watches (although, experiments have shown expert demos like this are still better than nothing). Effective modeling also includes expert think-alouds, where the person modeling explains what they are doing and why as they do it.

For example, while modeling how to put sheets on a bed, someone might say, "First, I look at the fitted sheet and identify which is the short side and which is the long side. I put the short side on the top so the shape of the sheet matches the shape of the bed. If I try and put this on the long side, it won't fit. See?" This is more effective than silently slapping the fitted sheet on the bed and saying, "Got it?" for a few reasons.

To learn from modeling, learners need to notice key behaviors and store them in long-term memory. Expert think-alouds call attention to each of these key behaviors, making it hard for learners to miss them. Cognitive scientists call this process of thinking aloud while demonstrating "cognitive modeling."

Cognitive modeling is powerful because it unlocks access to expertise. It allows experts to make thought processes that are normally invisible, visible to novices. Learners can then use these decision rules when they try it on their own. It saves them from rigidly copying specific behaviors that may or may not apply in their context (e.g. "The stripes went horizontally when she put the sheet on her bed so that's what I'll always do."). If you recall what you've learned in previous chapters about the differences between expert and novice schemas, another way to say this is that think-alouds call the learner's attention to the deep structure of the task, so they are less likely to be distracted by surface features.

Cognitive modeling also helps learners self-regulate their learning. Listening to someone else verbalize their thought processes helps learners develop awareness of their own internal monologue (e.g. "I just remembered, I want to find the sheet's tag. I'm looking for it because I want it to be at the bottom of the bed so it doesn't touch me while I'm sleeping."). This "thinking about thinking" is known as metacognition, and it helps learners track their progress, monitor their effectiveness, and decide which strategy is helpful to use and when.

How Is This Different from Worked Examples?

In the last chapter, you read about worked examples. A worked example exists on a page or a screen as a completed product, which the learner must unpack. When you model how to do something, on the other hand, you are demonstrating the process in real time.

To be sure, there are similarities between the two. Both provide an example of expert performance. Both lighten cognitive load by giving the learner a process to use. This allows the learner to focus on executing accurately rather than using up all their working memory space trying to figure out what to do.

Despite their similarities, worked examples and modeling each have unique benefits. Worked examples are a great scaffold for learners when they try out something for the first time. For example, a learner can reference a worked example of someone else's code in a statistical software program as they try to write their own. If they had seen someone model how to write the code but didn't have a written worked example, they'd have to retrieve precisely what they saw and heard from long-term memory, which is unlikely after their first exposure. A worked example provides an artifact that eases the burden of having to commit everything accurately to memory right away.

Cognitive modeling, on the other hand, provides the learner with access to real-time decision making and self-regulation strategies in a way that worked examples cannot. If we return to learning how to change the sheets on a bed, providing a handout with a series of step-by-step pictures of how to put a fitted sheet on a bed shows the solution (worked example), but it doesn't necessarily help the learner know how to regulate their desire to start cursing when it seems like the sheet won't fit.

Modeling is also great to use when there are a lot of decisions sitting under each step of a process. Think back to what you learned about dual-channel processing in chapter 10. When you are trying to teach something with several steps and each requires lots of rationale, your worked example can end up a cluttered mess. You may actually cause cognitive overload with a complicated worked example because you are flooding the visual channel with diagrams, annotations, and words. Modeling allows you to offload some of that information to a different channel. The learner can watch the process unfold step by step (visual channel) while simultaneously listening to the rationale (verbal channel). With the information split across two channels, cognitive overload is less likely.

Modeling, Supercharged

Researchers have found a couple of ways you can make modeling especially effective.

Strategy 1: Prompt Processing about Key Behaviors

You've heard us say this several times before, but when learners actively process information, they are more likely to remember it later. After you've modeled how to do something, prompt the learner to engage in deep processing about each key behavior. This will make it more likely that what they learned sticks.

In Taylor and colleague's 2005 meta-analysis, they note that several experiments have focused on getting learners to generate "rule codes." Rule codes are names for the key behaviors in the model that the learner needs to store in long-term memory. For this to be effective, the learner should verbalize what the person was doing and *why* it matters. For example, if you were teaching your child how to take out the trash, after demonstrating you might ask, "What did I do first? How did that help? After that? Why bother with that?" This is similar to the prompts for self-explanation you read about in the last chapter on worked examples. In both cases, the goal is to get the learner to explain the underlying purpose of each step in a new process.

In a 2007 review, Schworm and Renkl examine experiments showing how rule codes are most effective when they are learner generated, as opposed to handed to the learner. However, the same studies show that learners struggle to generate these spontaneously. They need clear prompts guiding them (e.g. "In the how-to video, what was the purpose of the first step?" vs. "What were your takeaways from the video?")

Strategy 2: Employ Coping Models

There's another way to make your modeling more effective: Use what researchers call "coping models." Coping models include making mistakes and correcting them in real time. They often demonstrate how to refine a process by learning from errors and making fewer each time.

Let's go back to changing the sheets. If you wanted to model how to do this using a coping model, you might start by modeling a mistake, like putting the sheets on inside out. In a coping model, you'd catch yourself saying something such as "Wait, I just noticed the seam is sticking out. I need to turn these sheets right-side out." Then you'd quickly fix your mistake and continue.

Coping consistently outperforms error-free modeling in experiments for a few reasons. Remember the power of non-examples in chapter 4? The learner is exposed to common mistakes. They'll now know to avoid these in the future.

In a coping model, the learner also gets access to nuanced internal dialogue. When an expert demonstrates self-monitoring in this way, it builds novices' schemas for noticing errors and corrective rationale. They'll understand not only that this wasn't the right move but also *why*. Researchers also posit access to this type of internal dialogue may be part of what promotes self-regulation. Learners gain self-monitoring strategies, and it normalizes mistakes as part of learning process.

Modeling in Practice

Modeling can seem daunting. Let's look at how to make it effective, not awkward.

Big Idea: Show how to do something in real time. Make the implicit explicit so learners can quickly gain expertise.

Mental Model: The Bob Ross Effect.

Bob Ross had a show called *The Joy of Painting* that aired on public television from the mid-1980s to the mid-1990s. During the show, he would walk viewers through how to paint a landscape, while doing it in real time. Ross is a great guide when it comes to effective modeling. He consistently provided viewers with the two most important components of a strong demonstration.

Tip 1: Show What to Do in Real Time, Step by Step

The Joy of Painting was a show where you watched Ross paint in real time. He wasn't analyzing an existing painting to unpack the technique the artist might have used to create the clouds as would have been the case for a worked example. He also wasn't reading out instructions like "Drag a flat brush two inches from the top of the canvas horizontally for about three inches" and leaving it to the viewer to figure out how to translate this to their own canvas. Rather, viewers got to watch Ross mix colors, select the best brush for the job, and then paint clouds and then change elements of the landscape before their eyes.

These elements combined to give viewers a model that they could reference when they tried it on their own. As you know from the previous chapter, this lightens the cognitive load of the task. Rather than use up working memory capacity trying to figure out what to do, viewers had space to focus on painting that cloud effectively.

Tip 2: Make the Implicit, Explicit

Throughout *The Joy of Painting*, Ross described what he was doing ("We're going to put some tall pine trees in the foreground"), how to do it ("When you make the branches, it's almost like you are making a 'Z' with your brush"), and why ("We're using a darker color this time because these trees are in the shade of the mountain").

Ross's narration is a great example of making the implicit, explicit. As you know from the earlier sections of this chapter, unless the steps for how to do something are explicitly called out, learners may miss important ones ("We start by painting a base layer of white"). Learners also may not understand the rationale behind specific steps or their order ("A white base layer makes it easier to blend the layers of paint we'll add on top"). Making this explicit makes it more likely learners will be able to use the technique successfully on their own.

Ross was also known for saying, "Remember, there are no mistakes in painting, just happy little accidents." Earlier in this chapter we covered research that suggests access to modeling helps learners build self-regulation strategies. Showing viewers how an unintended brushstroke opened him up to new possibilities normalized mistakes as part of the painting process.

Ross regularly modeled making and addressing errors. For example, "I've made that darker than it would be if it were in the sun, so I'll just go back over it with a little paint thinner. There, it's back to how I imagined it." These coping models helped viewers avoid making similar mistakes and gave them strategies for fixing inevitable errors.

So you know that there are two things that are integral to effective modeling: 1) show what to do in real time, step by step, and 2) make the implicit, explicit. Let's take a look at what this might look like outside of *The Joy of Painting*.

Imagine one of your colleagues, Maisie, comes to you to let you know that someone who reports to her, Olivia, has resigned. Olivia shared she's leaving to "take some time for herself and her family." Because Olivia isn't leaving for a new opportunity, Maisie is concerned about how others on the team will react and is seeking guidance on when and how to share the news. This is a situation that lends itself to modeling because tone and affect are going to be as important as what she chooses to say.

Here's how you might reply if you were channeling your inner Bob Ross:

> Obviously, you'd want to meet with Olivia and align on all of this first but if it were me, I'd use time at your team meeting tomorrow to make the announcement to head off side conversations. I'd say something like, "Hey everyone, before we close out, we have a team announcement. I'm going to pass it to Olivia to share more."

> After Olivia shares with the team that she's leaving, have her pass it back to you so that you can celebrate Olivia's time here. You know what to highlight better than I do, but maybe something like, "During her time here, Olivia has led the creation of a new field guide, something our customers have been asking for for years. In addition to her excellent project management skills, part of what made the project successful was the way she kept our users at the center of every decision we made. Olivia, we are so grateful for the perspective you've brought to our team. It will continue to shape our work for years to come. Goodbyes like this are bittersweet. Obviously, as your colleagues, we are sad we won't get to work with you day to day anymore. And while we are sad for us, we are excited for you and can't wait to see what you accomplish in your future endeavors."
>
> I'd do that for two reasons. Passing it back to you means there's no opportunity for questions from the team that may invade Olivia's privacy. Celebrating her contributions with a warm tone and easy affect also tells the team that she's not exiting on bad terms. There's less grist for the rumor mill.
>
> Oops, just realizing I forgot, I wouldn't stop there. I would close by letting the team know what the plan is for backfilling her work. That way you head off anxiety about missed deadlines or team members who may become overloaded having to absorb Olivia's workstreams.
>
> So to recap, I'd have her share first, you follow with a celebration of her time, and you close with an update for the team on how her work will be backfilled.

What makes the way you shared your opinion helpful? The two components of effective modeling, of course.

First, you weren't talking hypothetically about what you might say. You modeled delivering the announcement in real time so Maisie could hear your tone and see your body language. Both will be key when she needs to share the news with her team.

You also made the implicit, explicit. You named the three steps of a departure announcement (e.g. "So to recap, I'd have her share first, you follow with ..."). You provided rationale for each step ("Celebrating her contributions with a warm tone and easy affect also tells the team that she's not exiting on bad terms"). By modeling a mistake ("Oops... I wouldn't stop there. I would close by letting the team know what the plan is for backfilling her work"), you help

Maisie see the implications of leaving that last step off (e.g. anxiety about missed deadlines or individuals having to take on more work).

Conclusion

Modeling is one of the most effective ways you can help someone learn something new. We've shared a few examples here, but you can use it in contexts ranging from how to change a tire to how to give hard feedback. You'll see its adaptability in the proliferation of how-to and tutorial videos on the internet that cover topics as diverse as: How to use new video editing tools; how to style your outfit; how to perfectly sear a steak; how to improve engagement during a social media campaign; and hair and makeup tutorials. We could continue listing topics indefinitely, because in almost any situation, you'll be better off showing someone what to do than just talking about it.

Takeaways

- Researchers have found that when they give people identical information – in one condition through modeling (someone performing a task) and in another by presenting key points (a list of important takeaways) – people learn more from modeling.
- The rationale behind why experts use the processes they do is often a mystery to novices. Cognitive modeling, where experts think aloud explaining what they are doing and why as they do it, helps novices access this information and learn more, faster.
- Coping models include making mistakes and correcting them in real time. They help learners avoid common errors, give learners strategies to correct course, and normalize mistakes as part of the learning process.

References and further reading

Decker, P. J. (1980). Effects of symbolic coding and rehearsal in behavior-modeling training. *Journal of Applied Psychology, 65*(6), 627–634.

De La Paz, S., Butler, C., Levin, D. M., & Felton, M. K. (2024). Effects of a cognitive apprenticeship on transfer of argumentative writing in middle school science. *Learning Disability Quarterly, 47*(2), 70–83.

Dodson, T. M. (2023). Effects of expert modeling videos on the development of nursing students' clinical competence. *Journal of Nursing Education, 62*(8), 454–460.

Dodson, T. M. (2023). Use of expert modeling videos in undergraduate nursing education: A systematic review. *Journal of Nursing Education, 62*(2), 89–96.

Franklin, A. E., Sideras, S., Gubrud-Howe, P., & Lee, C. S. (2014). Comparison of expert modeling versus voice-over PowerPoint lecture and presimulation readings on novice nurses' competence of providing care to multiple patients. *Journal of Nursing Education, 53*(11), 615–622.

Giaimo, C. (2017). *One of the earliest industrial spies was a French missionary stationed in China.* Atlas Obscura. Available at: www.atlasobscura.com/articles/porcelain-corporate-espionage-china-missionary-dentrecolles (Accessed: December 17, 2024).

Hoogerheide, V., van Wermeskerken, M., Loyens, S. M., & van Gog, T. (2016). Learning from video modeling examples: Content kept equal, adults are more effective models than peers. *Learning and Instruction, 44*, 22–30.

Hvistendahl, M. (2019). *The oldest game.* Foreign Policy. Available at: https://foreignpolicy.com/2019/04/27/the-oldest-game-industrial-espionage-timeline/ (Accessed: December 17, 2024).

Huang, X. (2017). Example-based learning: Effects of different types of examples on student performance, cognitive load and self-efficacy in a statistical learning task. *Interactive Learning Environments, 25*(3), 283–294.

Pedersen, S., & Liu, M. (2002). The effects of modeling expert cognitive strategies during problem-based learning. *Journal of Educational Computing Research, 26*(4), 353–380.

Schworm, S., & Renkl, A. (2007). Learning argumentation skills through the use of prompts for self-explaining examples. *Journal of Educational Psychology, 99*(2), 285–296.

Taylor, P. J., Russ-Eft, D. F., & Chan, D. W. L. (2005). A meta-analytic review of behavior modeling training. *Journal of Applied Psychology, 90*(4), 692–709.

Naval, E. (2019). *The curse of knowledge.* Available at: https://ucatt.arizona.edu/news/curse-knowledge (Accessed: January 2, 2025).

van Gog, T., Verveer, I., & Verveer, L. (2014). Learning from video modeling examples: Effects of seeing the human model's face. *Computers & Education, 72*, 323–327.

Walker, S. G., Mattson, S. L., & Sellers, T. P. (2020). Increasing accuracy of rock-climbing techniques in novice athletes using expert modeling and video feedback. *Journal of Applied Behavior Analysis, 53*(4), 2260–2270.

White, M. C. (2017). Cognitive modeling and self-regulation of learning in instructional settings. *Teachers College Record, 119*(13), 1–26.

Zimmerman, B. J. (2013). From cognitive modeling to self-regulation: A social cognitive career path. *Educational Psychologist, 48*(3), 135–147.

Zimmerman, B. J., & Kitsantas, A. (2002). Acquiring writing revision and self-regulatory skill through observation and emulation. *Journal of Educational Psychology, 94*(4), 660–668.

PART 5

JOURNEYS OF THE MIND: WHAT'S THE STARTING POINT, WHAT'S THE DESTINATION, AND WHAT'S THE BEST WAY TO GET THERE?

You've learned all the pieces of the learning process – but how do you put it all together? This section focuses on: setting objectives with schema in mind, sequencing to avoid cognitive overload, and focusing learners' attention on what's most important.

13. PREPARE FOR LAUNCH: SET OBJECTIVES FOR LEARNING

If the internet is good for anything these days, perhaps its highest value can be found in searching for those times when school-age children offer somewhat "misguided" answers to tasks set by their teachers, of which this is one of Jim's favorites.

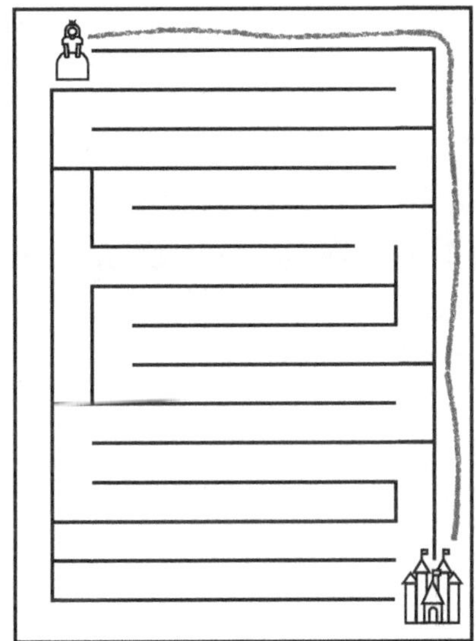

Now, there are a few ways to interpret what is actually going on here. It could be that the young person in question was not able to complete the task and therefore decided to take a playful "shortcut." Another interpretation is that this kid made an entirely earnest attempt at completing the task, but that the framing was muddled to the extent that "success" ended up being something entirely different than what was intended by the exercise.

This is true of adults, too. For instance, have you ever completed a phase of work only to learn that you were "successful," just not in the way that the situation actually called for? We all recognize these moments that might colloquially be called "finding answers to questions that weren't even asked," but why does this phenomenon occur in the first place and what can be done about it?

Even though poor task execution can be the culprit, it's often the case that such flaws are baked in at the outset as a result of poor objective-setting. We humans tend to be pretty good at *solving* problems (once the terms of the problem to be solved have been established). However, we are much worse at *setting* problems in ways that articulate exactly what others will need to know and be able to do in order to be successful.

Research into effective objective-setting acknowledges that learning is a "complex system." It rests on a fine balance between the things to be learned, the means by which things will be learned, and the eventual outcome of that learning. If the relationship between those components becomes imbalanced or disconnected, then the system is likely to fail in some way. Indeed, the stakes of such system failures are high, with organizations wasting countless hours and dollars on initiatives that are destined to fail before they have begun, precisely because they don't establish effective objectives for the type of learning and growth they hope to see.

The Science Behind Effective Objective-Setting

To understand how effective objectives can help, we first need to understand what they allow us to do. Thankfully, the relationship between objectives and performance is one of the most widely studied areas in all of psychology, with researchers showing time and again how effective objectives increase efficacy in performance across a whole range of domains, from organizational effectiveness, to academics, to sports.

Included in the many benefits of effective objective-setting are the following:

- **Effective objectives direct our activities** because they invite the learner (and the person in charge of the learning) to determine the precise focus of the learning and what will most likely result in that learning being successful.
- **Effective objectives regulate our expenditure of effort** because they tell us what will be the best use of our resources.
- **Effective objectives enhance persistence** because effort is more likely to continue until the objective is reached.

- **Effective objectives promote the development of new strategies for improving performance** because they provide a measure of excellence that can drive modification and continued refinement of the thing we want to improve.

So, if these are just a few of the benefits associated with effective objective-setting, how might we set about doing it ourselves? A solid starting point for thinking about objective-setting is to focus on *precision*. To get precise, ask yourself questions like:

1. What do I want people to know or be able to do as a result of this experience?
2. Under what conditions will people be expected to show what they know?
3. How will I know whether people have been successful?

Even though these questions are deeply intertwined, let's bucket them out into three categories and consider each in turn: Outcomes, conditions, and measures.

The Outcomes Component

Effective objectives are framed as specific, observable outcomes. One of the most robust and replicable findings in the psychological literature, with 90% of studies showing positive or partially positive results, is that setting specific, high goals leads to higher performance than simply urging people to "do their best." Doing one's best doesn't offer a picture of how to be better. Instead, we need to name the hoped-for outcome with precision.

Let's look at two examples to illustrate what we mean:

- **"Be able to present a structured argument on the benefits or dangers of artificial intelligence in a persuasive style"** is useful as an objective, because there are explicit characteristics that we know contribute to being able to perform that task (e.g. a contemporary knowledge of AI, knowledge of common structures for developing an argument, etc.). It's also observable. You could actually watch someone give a presentation and use that to determine whether or not they've met the objective.
- **"Become more persuasive,"** on the other hand, is less useful because it's vague. It would be hard to figure out what to prioritize as you support a learner in achieving this goal because it's hard to say what, specifically, they need to be able to do.

This approach to objective-setting also holds true with schema theory, which we explored at the beginning of 'Part 2: The Ordered Mind.' Decomposing the outcomes of a learning objective into specific knowledge and skills invites us to consider what specifically we want to ensure ends up in the learner's long-term memory and how those will fit into pre-existing schemas.

The Conditions Component

This component might not seem obvious at first, but we know from numerous studies that environmental factors shape performance. As such, we must take the conditions within which the performance is expected to occur into account whenever we set objectives for learning.

Research into the relationship between the tasks we set, the conditions within which they are undertaken, and the resultant performance has given rise to what is known as Parkinson's Law, which essentially states that effort is adjusted to the difficulty of a task. A famous 1975 study by Latham and Locke was one of the first to show this phenomenon playing out in the real world of work. In it, researchers observed the task orientation of loggers whose job it was to cut down and prepare trees for processing. The researchers found that the less time loggers had to cut and process the trees, the higher their rate of output. In other words, when the conditions of the work changed, the manner in which they went about the task changed accordingly. Similar studies have been conducted across a wide range of disciplines from chess to weightlifting, all of which show a similar moderating relationship between the conditional difficulty of a task and the resultant performance.

Even if we control for the knowledge to be acquired (i.e. the outcomes component we just explored), conditional factors have the power to transform performance into something unrecognizable for the person involved. For instance, imagine if we set the objective for you to run 100 meters in what would be a personal best time. The general conditions of that performance have the advantage of being pretty well established. We know how long 100 meters is, we know what your personal best is, and we could build a plan of strength and speed training that would move you toward beating your record. Now imagine I said that the 100-meter dash would be enacted on slick ice, uphill, in the face of high winds. Suddenly the preparation would need to shift because the conditions of the task have changed.

Let's return to our two examples to explore what the conditions component means:

- **"Be able to present a structured argument on the benefits or dangers of artificial intelligence in a persuasive style to your undergraduate classmates"** includes a useful conditional component since it communicates things that will help the learner prepare. They could, for instance, rely on the shared understanding of the topic in the room, since everyone in the audience would have engaged in the same arc of learning up to this point.

- Conversely, it would be quite another thing to say, **"Be able to present a structured argument on the benefits or dangers of artificial intelligence in a persuasive style to the United Nations,"** since the conditions of that performance would call on an entirely different set of capabilities (e.g. a contemporary understanding of the AI-related policies of different nations around the world, a range of examples illustrating how the benefits and dangers of AI have (or have not) been accounted for in those policies, etc.).

The lesson here is that conditions shape performance because the context modifies what's required to succeed. Whether we have control over performance conditions or not, we ought to consider them an integral part of setting objectives.

The Measures Component

This component considers the question: How will we know if someone has met our objectives? To answer this, we need a measure that aligns to the intended outcome.

In our experience, when we bring up measurement, there is often hesitation. This can come in a few forms. Some say, "We think data-informed decisions are important, but in our case, we aren't able to use a measure because ... [insert reason here: We don't have time, we don't have resources, what we are doing is too complex to be measured, etc.]" Others have had negative experiences with measures, often related to tests during their academic career, and don't want to recreate similar experiences for others. There is validity to all of these perspectives. *And* we want to make a case that, in spite of challenges and past experiences, a) it's worth the effort to draft a measure that is closely aligned to your objectives and b) administering the measure doesn't have to be a resource-intensive or negative experience.

How Measures Help

Prioritization

Measures help you prioritize. Let's return to the objective: **"Be able to present a structured argument on the benefits or dangers of artificial intelligence in a persuasive style to your undergraduate classmates."** An aligned measure of this objective might be a 10-minute presentation that will be evaluated by a rubric that includes categories drawn directly from the objective, such as:

- **Well-structured:** Presenter establishes the context of the issue, examines what is at stake, raises the oppositional point of view and responds with a counter-argument.

- **Persuasive style:** Presenter uses persuasive language. For example, evocative imagery and figurative language to paint a picture of the world if it were run by AI, or narrative structures such as the 'rule of three' to reinforce logical balance of the argument.
- **Aligned to audience:** Presenter appeals to undergraduate classmates' lived experience. For example, have them consider how AI might affect their lives for better or worse.

From here, it's easy to prioritize what you'll focus on in the course sessions leading up to this presentation: Structure, style, and audience. Knowing what you're measuring will help you make hard decisions about what to cut or keep in your syllabus. When your colleague sends you a hands-on activity to test out a new AI tool, you can acknowledge that it sounds both fun and generally related but make the hard decision *not* to use it. It isn't as essential to your learner's performance as what you are already planning to cover.

Professors with limited course sessions aren't the only ones having to make these tradeoffs. We live in a world where there is never enough time. There's a famous Peter Drucker quote: "What gets measured, gets managed." If the number of weeks to the project deadline are running out, the length of the client training is fixed, or the duration of board meetings is always three hours, knowing how you will measure the outcomes (even if you don't use the measure!) will help you make hard decisions about what to cut or keep.

A Tool to Evaluate the Objective

We often hear things along the lines of "What we are trying to do here is actually too complex to be measured." If you hear yourself saying this, you probably need to revise your objective. Take resources out of the picture for a moment. If there isn't a way to measure your objective, you probably haven't done enough to specifically define the outcomes and performance components listed above. Remember, beware the difference between a general goal ("Become more persuasive") and a specific, measurable objective ("Be able to present a structured argument on the benefits or dangers of artificial intelligence in a persuasive style to your undergraduate classmates").

This is also critical for the learner. A learner can use information from the measure to determine whether they have met the objective. Ask yourself: "Even if the learner has performed in a less-than-successful way, could they describe what they need to do to improve?" Ideally, your measure should provide information that allows you to answer, "Yes."

This ensures they don't get a grade on their AI presentation (or score on their mid-year review) and walk out saying, "I guess I could have done better." A clear measure allows them to look at their data and say, "I could have done better by more authentically acknowledging the opposing point of view before offering my own, rather than presenting the counterfactual as a strawman argument." This calls back to our earlier point about the limitations of "do your best" goal setting. Most of all, though, it shows how all roads lead back to the quality of the objectives that were set in the first place.

Usable Information

The main reason we need measures is they tell us whether or not we actually achieved our objectives. We can use this information to make future work more effective. Unfortunately, across a variety of fields, people tend to struggle with aligning measures to objectives.

Above we mentioned you could measure the objective "Be able to present a structured argument on the benefits or dangers of artificial intelligence in a persuasive style to your undergraduate classmates" using presentations and a rubric. Notice we didn't suggest asking "On a scale of 1 (not confident) to 10 (very confident), how do you feel about your ability to make a persuasive argument after completing this assignment?" or "Would you recommend this course to a friend?" It's not that measuring confidence or net promoter scores are wrong. They are simply aligned to different objectives (e.g. "Students will report increased confidence in their ability to make persuasive arguments"). You may choose to have multiple objectives, in which case you should choose a measure that is proximal to each.

Two questions to ask yourself when you determine the alignment of the measure to the objective (what researchers call "construct validity") are:

- Could someone perform **well** on this measure, even if they had **none** of the intended knowledge and skills?
- Could someone perform **poorly** on this measure, even if they had **all** of the intended knowledge and skills?

We'll start with the first question. Let's imagine we had gone with the measure "On a scale of 1 (not confident) to 10 (very confident), how do you feel about your ability to make a persuasive argument after completing this assignment?" Think back to the Dunning–Kruger effect we discussed in chapter 8. Research has repeatedly shown that people feel confident in their performance even when their actual skill is low. This isn't a good measure of the objective.

Now for the second question. This time imagine we used the measure "Would you recommend this course to a friend?" Their response could be driven by factors as wide ranging from "Yes, the professor bought us pizza on the last day of class" to "No, my friends are looking for easy As and this was a tough course." In the case of the latter response, even if the respondent had learned everything you hoped they would about making a persuasive argument, the score on the measure is low.

Aligned measures matter, because if we use faulty measures, we'll make faulty decisions from the data. In one series of studies conducted by Berton in 2012, researchers questioned the validity of a commonly used measure in marketing research called "advertising recall." When measuring advertising recall, researchers ask questions like "How often have you seen advertisements for this product? Where did you see them (e.g. billboards, television, magazine, internet, social media)?" In one study they found that even when participants saw an advertisement for the Ford F-150 once every 48 hours on television, on top of advertisements online and in magazines, more than one in four consumers reported no advertising recall. In another study, they found no relationship between advertising recall and purchasing behavior; for example, consumers reported almost zero advertising recall of an ad that drove an increase in sales by 15 share points.

The takeaway? Just because there is a commonly used measure, doesn't mean it's the right one. Alignment matters. If you are trying to measure the impact of an advertisement on purchasing behavior, you need to measure purchasing behavior (not advertising recall). If the companies in these studies had made decisions based on the data from advertising recall, they would have pulled the ads and lost out on sales.

Here's an additional word of caution. Research across a variety of fields (advertising, leadership, public policy, education) has shown that self-reports are often more correlated to characteristics of the respondent (e.g. personality, mood, and demographics) than their actual experiences. Researchers have also found low correlations between satisfaction and learning, and self-reported learning and actual learning. Self-reports of course have their place, but they are best suited to measuring changes in perception, not observable phenomena.

This chapter began with the premise that effective objectives are an expression of the things we want a learner to know and be able to do as a result of the learning experience. A cognitive-science-friendly way of expressing this is to say: Effective objectives acknowledge how the information we want finds its way into (and ultimately back out of) a learner's long-term memory. All of which brings us to the mental model for this chapter.

Effective Objectives in Practice

Big Idea: Effective objectives acknowledge the expected outcomes, conditions, and measures of a learning process in order to best support the learner(s) at the center.

Mental Model: Prepare for Launch.

Why setting learning objectives is like preparing to send a rocket into space.

The business of launching millions of pounds of metal, fuel, and the occasional human into space requires a fair amount of planning and goal setting. Thankfully, there are some lessons from the process we can apply to creating effective objectives.

Step 1: The outcomes component = "Defining a successful launch." It's not enough to say that success is "taking off" when in fact there are myriad things the rocket needs to do in order for its launch to be considered successful.

Imagine that you have been tasked with planning a work retreat for your team. You start by sitting down to determine objectives. Consider the following options and compare the merits of each.

Option 1: The aims of this retreat are to build trust across the team and set a new strategic direction for our work together.

Option 2: By the end of this retreat, I want colleagues to be able to:

- Name the three highest-leverage strategic steps we will take over the course of the next 18 months.
- Identify at least two ways in which their existing roles and areas of expertise can contribute to our high-leverage strategic steps.
- Describe one growth area they will need to address in order to achieve the strategy and create a plan for growth in those areas.
- Identify the ways their "whys" for the work overlap and complement each other.

Comparing the two options: As you can see, **option 1** is more a case of wishful thinking than an articulation of a precise set of learning objectives. **Option 2,** on the other hand, names specifically what will be the product of the team's time together. It also acknowledges the team members involved, considers what they may already know (or need to know), and sets that against the work to be done. Finally, it avoids falling into platitudes like "build trust" and instead names what the process will actually look like. Anyone attending this retreat will have a clear understanding of what the aims and means of the experience will be. The specificity of the objectives will also make it easier to prioritize how people spend their time together.

Step 2: The conditions component = "Deciding the conditions within which a successful launch will take place." Success on a bright, cloudless day is differently considered than success in high winds and driving rain, hence rocket launches are abandoned when the weather isn't conducive.

Now imagine that you need to consider the environment in which the retreat will take place. What would you pay attention to and why?

Option 1: I would want to know whether the space is comfortable, will we have enough natural sunlight, and snacks... snacks are always important. I also know that a few of our team members are new, so they might need help finding the retreat center as they won't have attended an event there before.

Option 2: I know that in previous years we have vacillated between a multi-day, in-person retreat of 3–4 days versus carving out that same amount of time virtually, chunked over a three-week period. When I think about the trust-building work of comparing our "whys" for this project, the first option will reduce feelings of being rushed or distracted. My vote is that this should be uninterrupted and in person.

Comparing the two options: In this example, **option 1** considers context but does so in a superficial way. Of course, having a comfortable environment in which to work matters (as do snacks) but it's really difficult to draw a direct line between that and the stated objectives of the retreat. **Option 2,** on the other hand, acknowledges the relationship between the broad-based conditions of the work, those involved, and the work to be done. In this case, the difference between an in-person environment with dedicated stretches of time is clearly superior to that same time stretched out over a series of virtual sessions.

Step 3: The measures component = "Determining the extent to which the launch was a success." A rocket launch, like any complex process involving hundreds of people, relies on dizzyingly complex before- and after-action reviews so that everyone involved can determine whether and how their part in the process was successful.

Now imagine that the retreat is coming to an end. How will you know whether you have achieved your aims? What approach would you take?

Option 1: At the end of the retreat, I would sit everyone in a circle and ask them to share their thoughts on the following prompt: "I used to think, but now I think." I would then invite them to email me a reflection in which they express the most useful thing they took from the retreat, along with suggestions for how to improve it next time.

Option 2: At the end of the retreat, I would build in time for attendees to individually respond to a series of questions. These could include:

- How would you describe three highest-leverage strategic steps we established over the course of the retreat? In what ways do you feel your existing role and expertise can best be employed to meet those aims?
- In order to meet those aims, what's one growth area you want to identify and how will you address it? How can I and others in our team best support you in achieving that growth?
- As a result of the "why" exercise, what common traits did you see across our team and what did that tell you about the purpose we share in this work?

Comparing the two options: Here, **option 1** treats the close of the retreat as an opportunity to reflect, but since the objectives established at the beginning were so vague, so are the means of reflection. Team members could engage in this step without connecting any part of their reflection to the intended purpose of the experience. By contrast, **option 2** offers specific questions that map back onto the objectives. Anyone answering these questions would know whether the retreat met its aims and the extent to which they as attendees were successful.

Conclusion

Whether you're launching a rocket or planning a retreat, it's fair to say that the likelihood of success has in large part been established before the countdown has even begun. The way we define success, the environment in which we intend to operate, and the metrics we use are all factors critical to any learning experience.

The good news is: By establishing precise, thoughtful objectives, we can marshal these factors into productive alignment and set a successful launch for the learning to come.

Takeaways

- Setting effective objectives is seen to have a number of benefits for learning, with research showing how effective objectives increase performance across a range of domains.
- Effective learning objectives ought to consider performance, conditions and outcomes, and key components of the process:
    - **The outcomes component** states that objectives should be framed as concrete goals with explicit parts that contribute to the hoped-for outcome.
    - **The conditions component** states that environmental factors shape performance, so we must take the conditions within which the performance is expected to occur into account whenever we set objectives for learning.
    - **The measures component** considers how well someone would have to perform to be considered competent in the thing they set out to learn, and does so by setting standards for performance and by offering a means by which the learner can tell when they have met or exceeded those standards.

References and further reading

Barnett, P. (2015). If what gets measured gets managed, measuring the wrong thing matters. *Corporate Finance Review, 19*(4), 5–10.

Behn, R. D. (2003). Why measure performance? Different purposes require different measures. *Public Administration Review, 63*(5), 586–606.

Berton, R. (2012). Marketers who measure the wrong thing get faulty answers. *Business Review, 85*(2), 117–128.

Biggs, J. (1995). Assessing for learning: Some dimensions underlying new approaches to educational assessment. *Alberta Journal of Educational Research, 41*(1), 1–17.

Bloom, B. S. (1965). *Taxonomy of educational objectives: The classification of educational goals.* New York, NY: David McKay.

Cohen, J., & Berlin, R. (2020). What constitutes an "opportunity to learn" in teacher preparation? *Journal of Teacher Education, 71*(4), 434–448.

Cook, D. A., Brydges, R., Ginsburg, S., & Hatala, R. (2015). A contemporary approach to validity arguments: A practical guide to Kane's framework. *Medical Education, 49*(6), 560–575.

Cook, D. A., Zendejas, B., Hamstra, S. J., Hatala, R., & Brydges, R. (2014). What counts as validity evidence? Examples and prevalence in a systematic review of simulation-based assessment. *Advances in Health Sciences Education, 19,* 233–250.

Gagné, R. M., Briggs, L. J., & Wager, W. M. (1992). *Principles of Instructional Design* (4th ed.). Orlando, FL: Harcourt Brace Jovanovich.

Gronlund, N. E. (1970). *Stating Behavioral Objectives for Classroom Instruction.* London: Macmillan.

Latham, G. P., & Locke, E. A. (1975). Increasing productivity and decreasing time limits: A field replication of Parkinson's law. *Journal of Applied Psychology, 60*(4), 524–526.

Locke, E. A. (1968). Toward a theory of task motivation and incentives. *Organizational Behavior and Human Decision Processes, 3,* 157–189.

Locke, E. A., & Latham, G. P. (1985). The application of goal setting to sports. *Journal of Sport Psychology, 7*(3), 205–222.

Mager, R. F. (1962). *Preparing Instructional Objectives.* Belmont, CA: Fearon.

Pollock, E., Chandler, P., & Sweller, J. (2002). Assimilating complex information. *Learning and Instruction, 12*(1), 61–86.

Porter, S. R. (2011). Do college student surveys have any validity? *The Review of Higher Education*, *35*(1), 45–76.

Schön, D. A. (1992). *The Reflective Practitioner: How Professionals Think in Action*. Abingdon: Routledge.

Shondrick, S. J., Dinh, J. E., & Lord, R. G. (2010). Developments in implicit leadership theory and cognitive science: Applications to improving measurement and understanding alternatives to hierarchical leadership. *The Leadership Quarterly*, *21*(6), 959–978.

von Bertalanffy, L. (1968). *General Systems Theory*. New York, NY: Braziller.

14. READY PLAYER ONE: STRUCTURING AND SEQUENCING IDEAS

A friend of Jim's was learning to fly when the instructor, who was seated in the cockpit alongside, requested that the novice perform a seemingly straightforward operation. Unlike previous occasions when flying conditions were optimal, today's weather made for poor visibility. As a result, not only was the fledgling pilot unable to comply with his instructor's request, he later said that: "If you had asked me what my own name was at that moment, I'm not sure I would have been able to tell you."

Thankfully, the instructor was there to take control and avert any potential disaster but what exactly happened in that moment? Why did the novice freeze and why can we all point to similar moments of cognitive paralysis? Though he didn't have the terms to describe it at the time, his lack of preparedness meant he experienced a case of cognitive overload (a concept we covered back in chapter 9) that left him unable to engage in even rudimentary tasks. In other words, the amount of new stuff he was trying to do at once, combined with all the new features in his environment, was too much for his mind to bear.

Compare this to the experience of being in a flight simulator, in which a range of scenarios can be "dialed up" and their degree of difficulty managed and distributed according to where the learner is in their development. In this case, the simulator supports the learner by breaking down the difficulty of the task into a more manageable form. It also primes the learner by building upon what the learner already knows to support the learning to come. In this case, if the simulator had provided Jim's friend with opportunities to practice in low-visibility conditions before he had to encounter them in real life, then the cognitive freeze he experienced could have been avoided. He would have been able to manage his cognitive load rather than be controlled by it.

Well, it turns out the flight simulator has lessons for how we acquire any new knowledge or skill. Instead of waiting for learners to become overwhelmed by conditions or content, we can structure and sequence the presentation of information in ways that maximize learning, without the often-paralyzing effects of information overload.

What Is Structuring and Sequencing and Why Does It Matter?

As explored in chapter 2, we know that the information we commit to memory isn't learned in isolated units but rather in the form of interconnected networks known as schemas. We also know from chapter 9 that working memory is notoriously limited and, as such, we must manage the cognitive load of learners as they integrate new information into their long-term memories. With all this in mind, it becomes important to ask: "How can I structure and sequence ideas to better align with the way people organize information in their minds?"

Priming the Learner for Learning: The Importance of Prior Knowledge

One thing we know for sure is that prior knowledge helps us to manage cognitive load. As such, it's crucial to consider the role that existing understanding plays whenever we introduce new information to a learner. To illustrate how this works and why it matters, consider a thought experiment, adapted from the work of cognitive scientist Dan Willingham.

Try to remember the following list of letters: **BB CA NSAC IANA TOU NI CEF**
Now try the same with this list of letters: **BBC NASA CIA NATO UNICEF**

Why was one easier to remember than the other? Because you already knew the acronyms in the second row. It lightened the cognitive load so that you only had to remember five chunks of recognizable letters rather than a jumble of 20 disassociated letters. The same is true for any learner: The more relevant prior knowledge, the lighter the cognitive load will be.

This phenomenon plays out in the research. In one series of experimental studies on the importance of pre-training, conducted by Mayer and Moreno in 2003, groups of students were shown videos involving narrated animations about how brakes and pumps work. The students who were provided with advanced priming on the names and functions of the parts that make up pumps and breaks *before* watching the video performed better on subsequent problem-solving tests than those who did not. Knowing the names and individual functions of the parts in advance lightened the cognitive load. All these learners had to focus on while they watched the videos was the *relationship between* the parts and how they make the pump or brake system work. Meanwhile, learners from the other group had to try to track the name of each part, their individual function, and how the relationships between the parts contributed to the functioning of each machine – all of which led to cognitive overload.

K. Anders Ericsson (whose work on deliberate practice we covered in chapter 8) had many of these ideas about prior knowledge in mind when developing his influential paper on expert performance. In his 1993 study, Ericsson offers us an elegant picture of the relationship between prior knowledge and performance, which he refers to as *memory skill*. For Ericsson, memory skill is the ability of experts to "rapidly access relevant information in an extended working memory that relies on storage in long-term memory," which in turn enables them to "circumvent the limited storage capacity of short-term memory."

For instance, the reason a master chess player can make faster, better moves than you or I isn't because their working memory is any more advanced than anyone else's. It's because they have a vast repertoire of moves in their long-term memory upon which they can rely. Think about how in the earlier example the acronyms made it easier to remember the letters because they "chunked" the information. Chess masters do the same thing. Expert chess players aren't thinking about individual pieces. They can recall a move (and the accompanying board configuration) as one "chunk" of information. They play faster than novices because when they see the pieces on the board, they can draw on *all* the occasions when they have seen a similar scenario and immediately pull the relevant move to mind. By contrast, a novice presented with the same game play would be busy trying to reason their way towards the next best move, while considering every individual piece. This takes longer and sends cognitive load sky high.

This is also why the well-worn refrain "students don't need to commit things to memory anymore, they can just Google what they need to know or use AI to help them write" is so infuriating to anyone who understands how learning happens. Background knowledge is a *required* part of what is often termed expertise, problem-solving, creativity, innovation, or critical thinking. Or as Dan Willingham puts it: "Understanding is remembering in disguise."

Paying Attention to the Parts and the Whole

As we have already seen, choices about how to present information have significant implications for cognitive load. Cognitive scientists refer to two specific modes for organizing information as *isolated* or *interacting* – and here's how each plays a part in the learning process.

- **Isolated elements:** This means presenting one piece of information at a time without showing how those pieces of information fit together – also known as a "part-task" structure.
    - e.g. Imagine you were a naturalist leading a tour in the Serengeti and wanted to prime participants for what to expect from the wildlife they will encounter. Presenting that information as isolated elements would look something like seeing an animal in the distance (there's a wildebeest, there's a crocodile) and then providing people with just-in-time information about that species, repeating this each time a new animal comes along.
- **Interacting elements:** This means presenting all information at once in order to show how the parts fit together – also known as a "whole-task" structure.
    - e.g. Imagine you're that same naturalist but now you take a different tack that involves presenting a more holistic picture of the ecosystem and how the different species interact with one another and their environment. You might say, "This watering hole is a favorite of wildebeest in the area, but it's also filled with crocodiles, so expect to see some crocs creeping their way towards their prey as the herd of wildebeest start to drink."

Notice here how one example sees the various species in isolation and only provides the information as it is needed, while the other aims to offer an integrated picture in which all the pieces (and the relationships between them) matter.

In a 2002 study, Pollock, Chandler and Sweller sought to understand whether presenting isolated elements or interacting elements of information led to better learning outcomes. The study mixed up the methods into different combinations (e.g. all isolated, all interacting, or a combination of the two). It turned out that optimal learning resulted when both were in play, as long as the *sequence* was carefully considered.

Specifically, experiments showed that *isolated* elements were best presented at the outset of the learning experience and *interacting* elements were best presented later on. This finding again supports the hypothesis that whenever novice learners are presented with complex information, it pays to first present it in an isolated form since that spreads out the cognitive load required to process all that new information (e.g., before you head out for the tour, review images and names of animals you'll likely see). At the same time, since we know from our understanding of schemas that it's important to "connect the dots" between parts of information, there must ultimately come a time when an *interacting* elements approach is required so that learners can see the whole picture and not just parts of it.

This is where the work of K. Anders Ericsson comes back into play. Ericsson studied violin students at the Music Academy of West Berlin who had the potential for careers as international soloists. This already placed them in an elite bracket in performance terms, so Ericsson sought to understand what was happening in cognitive terms. Of the many factors identified in the students' success (among them the deliberateness of the practice undertaken and the significance of motivation and effort), Ericsson noted along the way how "the instructor has to organize the sequence of appropriate training tasks and monitor improvement to decide when transitions to more complex and challenging tasks are appropriate."

This is why you can't hand a first-grader a Bach concerto, wish them the best of luck, and walk away. In reality it is the careful, incremental progression from foundational to complex tasks that wins the day. For example, you must start with how to play simple notes, then learn to pluck, then bow, then put all that together into basic songs like "Twinkle, Twinkle Little Star," and so on.

We now know why it would be futile to do one before the other, because any novice player will experience cognitive overload if they are trying to figure out how to hold the bow, at the same time as where to place their fingers to make a note, at the same time as how to read music. It's more than their working memory can handle. For sophisticated performance, the fundamentals had to have been long-ago automated and stored in long-term memory so that working memory could be freed up for focusing on highly technical fast-paced runs of notes or playing with appropriate expression.

This may seem obvious in the case of a first-grader with a violin. However, how many times have you heard someone complain about a team's "poor performance"? How often were the people on these teams actually provided with sequenced training and practice opportunities?

So, it turns out the only way to have our cognitive cake and eat it – so learners appreciate both the isolated and interacting elements of new knowledge – is to intentionally structure and sequence that process.

Knowing When and How to Offer Structured Support

You may be reading this thinking, "Rather than spend time pre-training, it will be more efficient to offer in-the-moment support." In reality, this "break glass in case of emergency" approach can end up doing more harm than good. Imagine, for instance, the difference between teaching someone to swim through a carefully sequenced series of lessons, versus throwing them in at the deep end, waiting for them to be on the verge of drowning, and only then shouting advice on what they should do to stay afloat. In this example, even though the aim is to help, the last thing this person needs is additional information with which to contend. This also bears out in the research, which shows that whenever learners experience cognitive overload, additional information added into the mix actually makes matters worse rather than better, even if that additional support is designed to assist the learning.

Thankfully, we know from research that effective structuring and sequencing bakes the means of support into the learning process itself. This means the learner gets what they need when they need it, rather than hitting them with new information at inopportune moments. This approach is variously known by cognitive scientists as "just-in-time" or "pay-as-you-go" processing. It calls on us to determine the cognitive load a learner must bear at any given moment in the learning process *without* becoming cognitively overwhelmed. A simple way of thinking about this is to consider the following two sentences created as a thought experiment by Jerome Bruner in his 1966 seminal work *Toward a Theory of Instruction*:

> "This is the squirrel that the dog that the girl that the man loved fed chased."
> "This is the man that loved the girl that fed the dog that chased the squirrel."

The important thing to note here is that these two sentences contain exactly the same information. So, what makes one almost impossible to read, and the other straightforward by comparison? It comes down to the logical progression of information in each case and the impact each has on our ability to manage the cognitive load of the information on display.

One way of thinking about these examples is to draw again on our friend K. Anders Ericsson and see effective sequencing is akin to providing a learner with the foundational, in-the-moment *memory skills* they need to move along each phase in an arc of learning (i.e. step B *must* come after step A because B *relies* on the understanding of A).

This is different to the concept of prior knowledge we explored in chapter 6, which operated under the assumption that relevant knowledge already existed and thus all we needed to do was activate it on the part of the learner. In this case, the knowledge a learner needs for each step is being *built as they go*, as a direct result of the sequencing choices being made on their behalf. All of which brings us to our next mental model.

Structuring and Sequencing in Practice

Big Idea: Working memory is limited, so we should sequence learning so that people get what they need before they are asked to apply it.

Mental Model: Ready Player One (or why sequencing information is a bit like a video game).

Step 1: The Aim of the Game

Most video games have established objectives in mind: Navigate the map, avoid danger, vanquish enemies. Whatever the aim, the game is unequivocal about what the player must accomplish and the rest of the player experience stems from that starting point – and so should this be true of laying the groundwork for a learning experience.

In fact, there's a reason why video games often start with that recognizable refrain: "Ready Player One." No game (or learning experience for that matter) is going to be playable if "readiness" is absent. In keeping with this premise, our first step rests on a simple question: "What is there to know and be able to do in order to be successful?"

Imagine for instance someone teaching their teenage son to drive a car. As anyone who has had this pleasure can testify, it's unwise to begin that process without first determining what it means to be a successful driver. Before even entering the car for the first time, you want to establish the goal. These should be fundamental (avoid running into other cars, stay in lane, keep both hands on the wheel, etc.), but we know they won't stay that way forever. In addition, you need to acknowledge that context is everything and that your goals will be contingent on where the action is taking place. For instance, if you were teaching your child how to drive in rural Idaho then that would call for a different set of goals than if you lived in Manhattan.

Step 2: The In-Game Tutorial

Most video games include a stage at the beginning that's designed to teach you the basics and walk you through the running, jumping, dodging, and striking moves you will need in order to win, and you can draw on this same strategy when supporting any learner. For this step we therefore ask another fundamental question: "What missing knowledge and skills would prevent someone from being able to do the thing(s) you want them to do later?"

In our example, an answer might be "you can't stop at a stop sign if you don't know where the brakes are." To build this and other foundational knowledge, you would probably walk the novice driver through the fundamentals while the car is still stationary so that they have an understanding of the necessary parts *before* they start driving the car. You might mark the location of the brake and the accelerator; show them how to activate the turn signal; or practice adjusting the mirrors – the idea being that (just as was the case with the study into pre-teaching trainees on the parts making up the pumps and breaks) any prior learning will lighten the cognitive load they will need to bear once they begin driving for real.

Step 3: Leveling Up

Video games are exceptionally good at sequencing the content a player will need to know in the right order. For instance, if a video game expected us to know how to defeat the final boss upon playing it for the first time, cognitive overload would reign, and gamers would walk away due to the unmanageable complexity they faced. Instead, even the earliest game designers came up with the idea of *levels*: An ingenious means by which the things a player ought to know can be sequenced. This way playing through any level of the game provides us with incremental support that will assist us in subsequent levels. In keeping with this premise, for this step we can ask: "Would someone be able to do Y without first knowing how to do X?"

Back to our ongoing example, the best way to level up would be through an incremental increase in difficulty. That is to say, start by driving in a parking lot to nail down the essentials, then graduate to a quiet street, then head onto the motorway. The key here is to treat each level of difficulty as the precursor to the subsequent level, such that completing X (the parking lot) provides the learner with enough of a grounding in the fundamentals to take on Y (the quiet street) and so on.

To supercharge the leveling-up process, you could think about incremental increases in difficulty in relation to *isolated* versus *interacting* elements. For instance, during the stationary phase you might first expect the learner to consider each of the pieces in isolation (e.g. here's the mirror, here's the signal, here's the steering wheel) before graduating to seeing these as parts of an interacting whole (e.g. merging across lanes and exiting a motorway requires checking your mirror, activating the turn signal, and executing the maneuver as an integrated series of moves rather than a series of isolated steps).

Conclusion

Whether you're playing a video game or teaching someone how to drive, we hope this chapter underscores the critical importance of structuring and sequencing any developmental experience. In much the same way that we wouldn't put the roof on a house until we have built the walls, and wouldn't add the walls until we had built a foundation: Order matters.

If in doubt, ask yourself what the aim of the game is, consider what the learner will need to know and be able to do in order to succeed, and then incrementally structure the experience so that succeeding in one step lays the foundation for succeeding in the next.

Takeaways

- We know that working memory is finite, so presenting learners with too much information at once will likely lead to cognitive overload. We can avoid this by the way we structure and sequence the information we present to learners.
- We can build "memory skill" in learners by: Determining what the overall goal of the learning will be; identifying what missing knowledge and skills would prevent someone from being able to meet that goal; and moving the learner along an arc of incremental increases in difficulty.
- Structuring and sequencing can also be improved by presenting isolated elements (standalone knowledge items) first and interacting elements (interconnected knowledge items in relationship with one another) later.

References and further reading

Agodini, R., Harris, B., Atkins-Burnett, S., Heaviside, S., Novak, T., & Murphy, R. (2009). *Achievement Effects of Four Early Elementary School Math Curricula: Findings from First Graders in 39 Schools.* NCEE 2009–4052. National Center for Education Evaluation and Regional Assistance.

Brophy, J., & Good, T. (1986). Teacher behavior and student achievement. In M. C. Wittrock (ed.) *Handbook of Research on Teaching* (3rd ed.). New York: McMillan.

Brown, M. C., McNeil, N. M., & Glenberg, A. M. (2009). Using concreteness in education: Real problems, potential solutions. *Child Development Perspectives, 3*(3), 160–164.

Bruner, J. S. (1966). *Toward a Theory of Instruction.* Cambridge: Harvard University Press.

Ericsson, K. A., Krampe, R. T., & Tesch-Römer, C. (1993). The role of deliberate practice in the acquisition of expert performance. *Psychological Review, 100*(3), 363–406.

Mayer, R. E., & Moreno, R. (2003). Nine ways to reduce cognitive load in multimedia learning. *Educational Psychologist, 38*(1), 43–52.

Newell, A., & Simon, H. A. (1972). *Human Problem Solving.* Englewood Cliffs, NJ: Prentice Hall.

Pollock, E., Chandler, P., and Sweller, J. (2002). Assimilating complex information. *Learning and Instruction, 12*(1), 61–86.

Smith, L. R., & Sanders, K. (1981). The effects on student achievement and student perception of varying structure in social studies content. *The Journal of Educational Research, 74*(5), 333–336.

Sweller, J., van Merriënboer, J. J. G., & Paas, F. G. W. C. (1998). Cognitive architecture and instructional design. *Educational Psychology Review, 10,* 251–296.

Willingham, D. T. (2009). *Why Don't Students Like School? A Cognitive Scientist Answers Questions about How the Mind Works and What It Means for the Classroom.* San Francisco, CA: Jossey-Bass.

Ziegler, J. C., Bertrand, D., Lété, B., & Grainger, J. (2014). Orthographic and phonological contributions to reading development: Tracking developmental trajectories using masked priming. *Developmental Psychology, 50*(4), 1026–1036.

15. FINDING YOUR WAY: FOCUSED ATTENTION

Book twelve of the Odyssey sees Odysseus and his crewmates leave Circe's island to continue their long journey home. Before their departure, Circe warns the sailors of three challenges they will soon face: The wandering rocks that will threaten to dash their ship, the monstrous Scylla and Charybdis between which they must carefully plot their course, and perhaps most infamous of all, the Sirens.

The songs of these winged temptresses are sweet enough to lure unwitting sailors to their death. So Circe proposes a strategy: Plug the crew's ears with beeswax so that they won't fall into the sirens' seductive trap. For Odysseus, whose curiosity often gets the better of him, the opportunity to hear the sirens' song proves too much to resist, so he asks his crew to lash him to the mast until the temptation passes.

As evidenced by this and myriad other encounters, the Odyssey wouldn't be much of, well, an odyssey without the influences of temptation and distraction faced by its cunning protagonist and crew. In his book *We Followed Odysseus*, modern-day sailor Hal Roth reminds us that, even though the distance between Troy and Ithaca is around 565 nautical miles, it is estimated that Odysseus sailed several thousand miles over the course of the 10 years it took to reach his destination.

Even though such diversions make for ripping yarns and epic tales, we have come to know that distracting people from the intended course is not necessarily conducive to learning. That is to say, if you want to learn something well, any phenomena that could take your attention away from the goals are unlikely to help. Luckily, like Circe's suggestions to Odysseus and his crew, there are strategies we can use to limit the ill effects of siren-like distractions and keep the ship of our attention pointed true at its course. The act of managing people's attention for effective learning will be the subject of this, our final chapter.

The Fundamentals of Attention, Distraction, and Learning

In the previous two chapters, we thought about the start- and end-points of a learner's experience. But having a great set of goals and a well-thought-through sequence for learning does not guarantee success. Unless you pay good mind to the role that attention and distraction play, the process can still go awry. For the last of our chapters, we will focus on getting learners from A to B in the least circuitous way.

As we have already explored a few times, most notably in chapter 9, we know that people's working memories are finite and learners can easily experience cognitive overload if we present them with too much information at once. It's also true that attention itself is a finite resource. We have to direct people's attention so that they focus on the information we want them to remember and not other things.

The problem is, the world is already full of potential distractions, and humans have a funny way of creating more of them as we try to convey information. Our attempts to make learning experiences more engaging often distract learners from the goals of the task. Cognitive scientists refer to these shiny but ultimately superfluous components as *seductive details* – and once you see them, it's rather difficult to unsee them.

Consider, for instance, your own experiences of school and you will likely recall a host of *seductive detail* moments. You may have dressed up as a centurion when learning about ancient Rome, built a diorama based on the setting of an Edgar Allan Poe short story, or designed a menu to help with French vocabulary. Despite the fact that you may remember those standout moments more than the run-of-the-mill days you spent at school, in order to know whether seductive details were at play you must ultimately ask yourself: "Are the things I recall actually connected to the content my teacher wanted me to remember, or were these details tangential to the core content to be learned?"

If the answer to this question is "the latter" then it's likely that all you got to experience and remember was how to dress like a centurion (rather than better understanding life in ancient Rome); build a diorama (rather than appreciating Poe's use of setting in his stories); or color in a lunch menu (rather than remembering that the French word for raspberry is *framboise*).

Indeed, throughout our time working with K–12 schools and in higher education, we have encountered numerous examples in which the (albeit commendable) instinct of educators to "engage" their students leads to an overreliance on the shiny over the substantive – or as one mentor of Jim's used to say: "Like a lighthouse in the desert: Brilliant but ultimately useless." When you are planning an activity, ask yourself, what will people *actually* be using working memory for, the majority of the time? If it's not processing information tightly aligned with your objective, it's the wrong activity.

So, we know that seductive details exist and that they threaten to shift the attention of learners away from what we really want them to learn. But what actually occurs at the cognitive level when our attention is affected, and what steps can we take to prevent that from happening?

How Our Attention is Compromised by Seductive Details

Researchers have consistently shown how easily attention can be drawn away from what matters in favor of what doesn't. Several studies also show how learning is significantly reduced for people who encounter seductive details compared to people who receive the same content without such distractions. From that research, cognitive scientists have identified at least two flaws in attention that seductive details can exploit: *Attention distraction and attention diversion.*

Attention Distraction

The first of these impediments to attention is akin to the examples we explored earlier, in which the learner's attention is distracted from rather than directed towards the intended content. Specifically, attention distraction plays on our tendency to be seduced by cognitively or emotionally interesting content that is tangential to the key content we're hoping to remember.

Interesting (But Ultimately Distracting) Content

This is content we might refer to as trivia, in that it serves as an intellectual trinket rather than contributing to an understanding of the main idea. For example, imagine reading the following text about the habitats of insects, which comes from a real 1997 study by Harp and Mayer:

> Some insects live alone, and some live in large families. Wasps that live alone are called solitary wasps. A Mud Dauber Wasp is a solitary wasp. Click Beetles live alone. *When a Click Beetle is on its back, it flips itself into the air and lands right side up while it makes a clicking noise.* Ants live in large families. There are many kinds of ants. Some ants live in trees. Black Ants live in the ground.

In this example and others like it, researchers showed how, even though participants rated the sentence in italics as more interesting, their recall of the relevant parts of the text as a whole was negatively impacted by its presence.

Conversely, participants who encountered the same paragraph with the seductive detail sentence removed were able to recall more of the main ideas of the paragraph. In other words, even though the fact that click beetles make a noise when flipping themselves back onto their feet is a cool thing to know, if what you want people to remember is the living conditions of different insects, then that shiny detail will likely impede the broader intentions of the learning.

Thinking back to the difference between experts and novices explored in chapter 3, we can now appreciate how experts would be more forgiving of such trivial details because their core knowledge allows them to move more fluidly between the less-relevant-but-shiny content and the stuff they need to take away.

Since the same can't be said for non-experts, we must take cognitively interesting content seriously and acknowledge its distracting properties. So, the next time you're preparing for a presentation, you might want to consider which aspects are the cognitive equivalent of "shiny objects" designed to distract rather than focus, and which parts are relevant to what you want people to take away.

Attention Diversion

Attention diversion is referred to by cognitive scientists as *schema interference*, which should give us a clue as to how it affects the learning process. As explored in chapter 6, the manner in which we encounter information is shaped by our existing schemas, such that we come to understand new things by reference to what we already know.

Research has shown that, whenever attention diversion happens, learners activate prior knowledge that is inappropriate or redundant to the intended learning, thus diverting them away from an understanding of the core ideas we want them to take away. Well-known instances of this can be found in the phenomenon of "false friends" that we encounter whenever we learn a new language. For instance, if I was trying to teach you about the Spanish word for a stuffy nose and I used the word *constipado*, then you could be forgiven for experiencing competing distractions that would take your attention away from the fact that I'm talking about someone with a cold. This is because that word activates entirely different schemas that relate to "blockages" affecting a different part of the body.

If left uncorrected, attention diversion (or schematic interference) can have long-lasting effects on future learning, since any new information will be encountered with that original misconception in mind. In this case, one can only imagine what might happen the next time the person in our example heads to the pharmacy with a blocked nose. In this sense, attention diversion is the thief that keeps on taking. Like a bug in our system, the inaccurate or irrelevant information activated in moments of attention diversion end up compounding over time.

As with attention distraction, we can easily imagine how attention diversion could sink a moment of communication before it has even begun. Imagine, for instance, you were presenting on customer retention. Now imagine that you opened with a slide that read "Never gonna give you up. Never gonna let you down."

Now, if your intention was to invite everyone in the room to start humming the 1987 pop hit *Never Gonna Give You Up*, then the opening of your presentation would have been successful. If, however, your aim was for everyone to walk away with five strategies to improve customer retention, it's likely that you would have cued everyone's long-term memory in ways that pull them away from the subject at hand and towards the redundant (albeit satisfying) tones of Rick Astley.

What to Do about the Attention Problem

We've illustrated the many ways in which our attention can be stolen, but how do we go about claiming it back? The most obvious response to this question is to remove the seductive details entirely – but unfortunately that's rarely enough. So, what else is there to do?

Researchers have spent time thinking about this as well, and have identified a number of evidence-informed approaches to focusing learners' attention in the face of competing distraction.

Have the Seductive Details Stand Apart

To say that seductive details impede learners from focusing on target content you want them to consider is very different from saying that such details are without value. Indeed, part of what makes learning fun are the nuggets of information you didn't expect to encounter but which make the overall experience fulfilling.

Thankfully, researchers have shown how you can have your seductive details cake and eat it, and it has something to do with how you slice and serve that information. In a 2005 study, Harp and Maslich were able to show that seductive details sprinkled throughout the delivery of content had more of a negative impact on learning than if those details were separated out from the rest of the material.

In other words, if you wish to include content that is interesting but non-essential, then consider presenting it as a side dish to the main meal. It could be that the seductive detail serves as a pithy, engaging introduction to the content, or as a thought-provoking conclusion. You could also use small but significant design choices to separate content out into its own text box or thought bubble so that it remains apart from the core components. Whichever strategies you adopt, the key is to make clear what's relevant and what isn't, and separate the two.

Cue Learners Towards Relevance

You likely recall with delight the comprehension questions featured in standardized tests and the like that you were required to take throughout your schooling years. Designed to determine what you understood about a passage or body of content, such questions tended to be asked *after* the act of reading. Though obviously useful as a means of testing for understanding, researchers have come to understand through careful experimental design that we can use pre-ordained questions or instructions to cue people towards the information we want them to engage in *before* they encounter the material at hand.

In a 1977 study led by Pichert and Anderson, researchers presented participants with a text about a house in which two boys were playing. In addition to recounting the games the boys played, the text included descriptive details about the house itself. Participants in the study were then primed according to three different conditions: The first group was asked to read the text as though they were someone interested in buying the house, the second group was asked to read the text as though they were someone interested in stealing from the house, and the third group was not given any stance to consider.

When researchers later asked participants to recall aspects of the text and compared each of the two treatment groups to the unprompted group, researchers discovered that the "buyers" were more likely to remember aspects of the text that referred to the *condition* of the house (e.g. how recently it was painted) whereas the "burglars" were more likely to recall aspects of the text that referred to the *content* of the house (e.g. the expensive-looking stereo system).

This research showed that people's attention could essentially be primed to consider certain details over others, even by simply lending them a dispositional stance going into the experience. Researchers were also able to show how straightforward comprehension questions, if asked before reading as opposed to after, could cue readers even more specifically towards those parts of content that were most worthy of their attention.

All this is to say, the power you have to (and we use this word considerately) manipulate people's attention is much greater than you might imagine. Perhaps even more important is that *you will cue people to pay attention to certain things over others whether you intend to or not*, so it pays to be intentional about that process from the start.

One last note. You may be reading this and asking yourself, are they saying I should make things as boring as possible? The answer is a firm no. Learning should be engaging, affirming, and satisfying. Our point is that because working memory is limited, make sure that engagement is *in service of your goals*, not detracting from them, which brings us to the last of our mental models.

Directing Attention in Action

Big Idea: Attention is finite and the world is full of distractions, so we should cue learners towards the information we want them to understand and remember, as opposed to other things.

Mental Model: Herding Sheep.

Imagine that attention is like a flock of sheep: If left to its own devices it will meander every which way without purpose or direction – but thinking like an expert sheep farmer (assisted by a trusty sheepdog) can help as you marshal people's attention and direct it where you want it to go.

Let us be clear. We're not saying that "people are sheep" in this instance; rather that our *attention* can behave like unruly sheep and therefore needs to be marshaled accordingly.

Step 1: Plot Your Path

If you wanted to move a large herd of sheep from one place to another, you wouldn't jump straight into the act of herding without first plotting your route. In fact, farmers will use paths, gates, and pens to pre-determine where they want their sheep to go and the most efficient path to get there.

The same is true of marshaling people's attention. When it comes to plotting the course, you're very much in a "cutting across town" rather than "taking the winding coastal route" mode. As such, you need to ask yourself: "What's the most direct path people can take to arrive at the destination of new understanding?"

Herding sheep (or people's attention) isn't just about determining where they will go; it's about declaring where you *don't* want them to go. This becomes especially important if the general direction of travel has multiple competing paths that would draw them away from the intended route. To deal with this, you must differentiate between pertinent content and those seductive details that will otherwise play their distracting, disrupting, or deviating part.

Imagine, for instance, you were coaching a 7-year-old how to kick a football (or soccer ball for our US-based friends). Even with a clearly defined goal such as "learn how to strike the ball cleanly," one could still engage the learner in activities that are misaligned with that goal.

For instance, you might be tempted to include work on trapping the ball, or scanning the field, both of which are good things to have but not essential to this particular skill. Instead, in the case of our fledgling footballer, an aligned set of activities designed to achieve the goal might be expressed as follows: In order to get better at striking the ball cleanly, we're going to concentrate on three core components:

- Keeping your head down
- Planting the non-striking foot securely
- Moving the striking foot through the ball.

Notice how these activities form the straightest possible line to the outcome. They map onto key parts of the process, *in service of the goal*, so that you can focus the attention of the novice on those components *and not other things.*

As a side note, if you think that guarding against misaligned activities is the preserve of planning football training for 7-year-olds, think again. Countless times we've seen meetings, training sessions, and workshops go awry because the selected activities are ill-fitting or too general for the stated goals of the work. For example, if you want your team to better understand a specific client's need, a scavenger hunt where they gather facts from the client's website might be fun, but it's unlikely to get your team the specific information they need.

Step 2: Marshal the Direction of Travel

Aligning activities to stated goals is a good place to start but we also know that 7-year-olds tend to be, well, 7 years old, and that seductive details are basically their daily diet. As such, you need to consider how you will direct their attention towards the goal and away from all the things that could distract them from the path – which is where your "sheepdog" comes in.

Think of the sheepdog in this case as the nudges you will provide to cue the learners' attention away from redundant details and towards the things you want them to know and be able to do.

Since we know from the studies described earlier that we can prime learners' attention prior to learning, we can use "sheepdog" moves to manipulate the learners' expectations of what is to come and provide them with a lens for sorting the necessary from the unnecessary.

Achieving this requires you as the expert to take (at least temporarily) the majority of the agency in the process. For instance, this is not a time to ask the 7-year-old novice footballer, "Okay. Where do *you* think we should begin today?" Expecting them to know where they want their attention directed would be akin to asking the sheep where it wants to end up. A novice will not be able to determine what they're supposed to know, how they're going to know it, or what's most worthy of their attention along the way, so these establishing steps are yours to take.

Instead, it's better to say: "Okay, in this session, we're going to concentrate on kicking the ball really, really well. To do that, we're going to focus on three main parts to that process: Keeping your head down, planting your non-striking foot securely, and moving the striking foot through the ball. It might be tempting to look at your teammates or towards the goal to see where the ball is headed, but I want you to block all that out. For today, all we care about is: Head down, strong planted foot, strike through the ball."

From there, you can design the components of the task so that the only way for them to interact with it is by encountering what you want them to understand. For instance, you could start by pulling the goal entirely from the drill, thus removing the learner's temptation to lift their head up at an inopportune moment. You could also sketch out a box next to the ball as the landing spot for the planting foot, so that the kicker can see for themselves whether they have placed it in the correct place. Finally, you can ask them to freeze at the end of their kick and pay attention to the final position of their leg and foot. Is it beyond the ball? Did you strike all the way through?

This strategy isn't limited to acts of teaching and coaching youngsters. You can use similar techniques to ensure adults are focused on and actively processing the information you want them to. Let's say you are leading a session with 30 participants. If you ask questions to the group and call on whomever responds, you are likely only focusing the attention of the three to four people who volunteer to answer your questions. It's too easy for the others to succumb to the siren song of email, messaging, or running through their to-do list in their minds. Instead, each time you ask a question, ask participants to turn and discuss with a partner or write down their response somewhere you can see before bringing the group back together. You are herding the group so they stay focused on the content of the session and not the errands they have to do after work.

Conclusion

The old saying goes "It's not the destination, it's the journey." Nevertheless, we hope the lessons of this chapter illustrate that both matter equally. In order to move people towards new understanding, it's not enough to state a goal or even come up with activities aligned to that goal. You must consider the path that will join the two, acknowledge all the seductive details that could disrupt the journey, and nudge the learner in ways that make their engagement with the core material an inevitability.

In other words, if you can plot a clear path and enlist your inner sheepdog to herd the attention of the learner back to the desired points of focus, you'll be better placed to lead them where you want them to go.

Takeaways

- Attention is a finite resource, but we can direct people's attention so that they focus on the information we want them to remember.
- Seductive details can compromise attention and include: Attention distraction (cognitively and emotionally interesting content), and attention disruption (content that confuses and prevents learners from building a coherent picture).
- To address seductive details, consider setting seductive details apart, and instead cueing learners towards relevance and away from redundancy.

References and further reading

Harp, S. F., & Maslich, A. A. (2005). The consequences of including seductive details during lecture. *Teaching of Psychology, 32*(2), 100–103.

Harp, S. F., & Mayer, R. E. (1997). The role of interest in learning from scientific text and illustrations: On the distinction between emotional interest and cognitive interest. *Journal of Educational Psychology, 89*(1), 92–102.

Harp, S. F., & Mayer, R. E. (1998). How seductive details do their damage: A theory of cognitive interest in science learning. *Journal of Educational Psychology, 90*(3), 414–434.

Lehman, S., Schraw, G., McCrudden, M. T., & Hartley, K. (2007). Processing and recall of seductive details in scientific text. *Contemporary Educational Psychology, 32*(4), 569–587.

McCrudden, M. T., & Corkill, A. J. (2010). Verbal ability and the processing of scientific text with seductive detail sentences. *Reading Psychology, 31*(3), 282–300.

Garner, R., Gillingham, M. G., & White, C. S. (1989). Effects of "seductive details" on macroprocessing and microprocessing in adults and children. *Cognition and Instruction, 6*(1), 41–57.

Pichert, J. W., & Anderson, R. C. (1977). Taking different perspectives on a story. *Journal of Educational Psychology, 69*(4), 309–315.

Roth, H. (1999). *We Followed Odysseus.* Port Washington, WI: Seaworthy.

Sundararajan, N., & Adesope, O. (2020). Keep it coherent: A meta-analysis of the seductive details effect. *Educational Psychology Review, 32*(3), 707–734.

Sung, E., & Mayer, R. E. (2012). When graphics improve liking but not learning from online lessons. *Computers in Human Behavior, 28*(5), 1618–1625.

CONCLUSION

So, there you have it. We hope you enjoyed this humble trip through the world of cognitive science and its many applications. Over the course of these pages, we have explored the structural formation of our seemingly limitless long-term memory, contrasted that with the limitations of working memory, and shown how an understanding of the mind can reconcile this contradiction to create better conditions for learning and growth. Along the way, we have explored everything from the questions we ask, to the stories we tell; from the deliberate practice we engage in, to the prior knowledge we activate.

To make these principles more usable, we relied on mental models. As stated at the outset, these serve as a cognitive blueprint for action, and we now know that they can be improved if we pay them deliberate attention. We hope that focusing on these models means you won't leave daily acts of learning and growth to chance, but rather inform your choices with a rich understanding of the mind at work.

More than all that, we hope this book has illuminated the ever-present nature of cognition in our lives, especially once one has the eyes to see it. In that respect, cognitive science doesn't just help us better understand our minds, it helps us make better sense of our world.